The Dark History of the Occult

The Dark History of the Occult

Magic, madness and murder

Paul Roland

Picture Credits

This edition published in 2022 by Arcturus Publishing Limited
26/27 Bickels Yard, 151–153 Bermondsey Street,
London SE1 3HA

AD008794UK

Printed in the UK

Contents

Introduction

Talk of the Devil

'If the devil does not exist, and man has therefore created him, he has created him in his own image and likeness.'

FYODOR DOSTOYEVSKY
(RUSSIAN NOVELIST, 1821–81)

Introduction

I may be risking my immortal soul by stating for a fact that there is no devil, Satan, Beelzebub, Lucifer or Old Nick in this world or the next, but I am confident that my assertion will be borne out by the evidence that is presented in the following pages. I fear no contradiction – not even an appearance by the old boy himself – for it will be shown that the devil was a creation of the early Church and that all of his deeds are entirely man-made.

That is not to say that there is no evil in the world, for though the devil does not exist his disciples and acolytes are clearly all around us. It is with their diabolical activities and beliefs that this book is chiefly concerned. The devil, I argue, is a personification of the dark side of human nature, of our basest instincts, impulses and desires, which we seek to deny and disown by projecting them on to a mythical figure of our own making. On the other hand, God can be seen as the projection of our divine potential. Angels and demons are, therefore, symbolic of our divine attributes and aberrations, the vices and virtues which are continually in conflict within us.

It is highly significant that no one has claimed to have actually seen the devil in his traditional form, with horns and a tail, since the Middle Ages – no one of sound mind that is. Society's persistent belief in this malevolent cosmic entity is an insult to the intelligence, a remnant of the Dark Ages when fear, superstition, ignorance and bigotry reigned over reason. To believe in the devil is to deny our divine nature and that, if anything, should be a sin. It simply makes no sense to give credence to the idea that in this infinite universe, in which our world is less than a speck of dust, an evil omnipresent cosmic being could manifest as a man in order to tempt us into committing what our ancestors once considered sinful. Until we free ourselves from this fairy-tale figure and, more importantly, the fear of the unknown that he personifies, we will empower our fears to rule over us and limit our progress in this world.

How can I be so certain that the devil is a figment of our collective subconscious? Well, if there is a devil, a malevolent supernatural entity who is continually vying for possession of our souls, where is the evidence of his existence? It is certainly not in the Bible, the book that Christian fundamentalists quote so fondly.

THE POWER OF NAMES

In the beginning was the Word and the Word was power. In ancient civilizations writing was a sacred art reserved for priests and kings, so the written word acquired an aura of mystery.

It was widely believed that to know the names of the angelic hosts and the demonic hordes was to have power over them. To know the name of an enemy was to possess something potentially more lethal than the sharpest blade.

In the Old Testament and other sacred texts of the biblical era an adversary was invariably referred to by a generic term, typically 'a Satan', in the belief that the psychic connection would be weakened if their birth name was in common usage. This practice was also the origin of the commandment that made it a sin to take the name of the Lord in vain. For the Jews the personal name of God, Yahweh ('He exists'), was itself a magical invocation and was therefore commonly referred to indirectly as the Tetragrammaton, or the name of four letters. Only the high priest was permitted to whisper the sacred name of the Creator once a year on the Day of

Atonement. At all other times the Jews referred to their maker as Adonai (Lord) or Elohim (God). To know the personal name of the Creator and its correct pronunciation was to know the secret of creation itself, for according to the Torah (the body of Jewish law and teaching) the Word with which God created the universe was his own sacred name.

Understanding the true significance of that concept was a lifetime's study for the Kabbalists, the Jewish mystics who sought the secrets of life and death that they believed were encoded in the Torah. Judaism has both an exoteric (outer) and an esoteric (inner) teaching. The former comprises the customs and rituals which have been performed so often and for so long that their true meaning has been lost and the latter is the spiritual heart of the religion, which only the mystics claim to fully understand. The same duality applies to Christianity and to Islam. Those who adhere to none of these traditions, but who believe that there is a golden thread of truth common to them all, take the road less travelled, a road that divides into the Left and Right Hand Path of the occultist.

BLACK VS. WHITE

Genuine adepts of the Left Hand Path do not, of course, consider themselves to be black magicians, just as Satanists will not admit to being devil worshippers. They simply see themselves as the centre of the universe and they regard their own desires as being of greater importance than those of everyone else. Often they will dismiss the devil as a medieval superstition. One can imagine why. There is simply no room in the universe for two egos of that magnitude to coexist. But Satanism is a smokescreen for the genuine black magician who serves only one master – himself – and understands that magic itself is neither black nor white. It is merely a process for transformation that is brought about by exercising the will, empowered by the emotions. It is the intention behind the act that determines whether a magician is an adherent of the Left or the Right Hand Path and intentions are diabolically difficult to determine if one is playing the devil's advocate. Those who seek experience of the upper worlds in order to gain greater insight into the workings of the universe are clearly on a different journey to those who are self-serving and seek to subvert others to their superior will.

It is a curious fact that both the black magician and his benign brother purify themselves before participating in any ceremony and both appeal to God and the angels for protection when consecrating the sacred circle with which they surround themselves. Even the most devoted disciple of the devil knows that it is not their infernal master who commands the legion of demons but God. The mere utterance of His name is sufficient to restrain them from breaking into the circle and it will banish them whence they came at the ritual's conclusion.

Black magicians and white magicians share the same curiosity about the nature of existence and both understand the Universal Laws – which are based on the premise that every human being is a microcosm, a universe in miniature. To reveal the true nature of the universe, seekers first have to explore the symbolic landscape of their own psyche and then they have to possess the courage to face what they find there.

Chapter 1

Who is Satan?

'An apology for the Devil: it must be remembered that we have heard only one side of the case. God has written all the books.'

SAMUEL BUTLER

TWO FORMS OF KNOWLEDGE

From the dawn of civilization there have been two forms of knowledge: the practical intelligence of the artisan and the academic and intuitive wisdom of the adept. The first can be instilled through education or acquired by observation, while the latter can only be awoken by initiation into the Mysteries, which offers direct experience of a greater reality.

In the occult ('hidden') tradition, the Old Testament myth of Adam and Eve is interpreted as an incentive for every individual to partake of the fruit on the Tree of Life and so become aware of their true nature and divine potential. To realize that we are more than mere mortals is to be free from the fear of death and the tyranny of religious diktats and dogma. It is significant that this inducement was articulated by the serpent, which has traditionally been a symbol of wisdom.

'Ye shall not surely die: for God doth know that in the day ye eat thereof, then your eyes shall be opened and ye shall be as gods, knowing good and evil.'

Genesis 3:4–5

But in the 'official' version of the story, as told by theologians, the snake is recast as a trickster who tempts Eve to eat the forbidden fruit so that man will be exiled from heaven and will thereafter be entirely dependent upon religious authority for absolution. That deliberate undermining of our divine nature and potential is surely the real original sin.

SATAN AS GOD'S ADVERSARY

Satan's first appearance in Judaeo–Christian mythology can be found in the Old Testament Book of Job, where as the angel 'ha-satan' he is assigned the task of testing the extent of Job's faith. In Hebrew, *ha-satan* translates as 'the tempter' or 'the accuser', an angelic being who is not by nature evil but is the one who identifies those on earth who are responsible for evil acts and who informs on those who have turned away from the Lord.

In the Torah, the Hebrew Book of the Law, 'satan' is an appellation that is used to denote any historical figure who is opposed to the Semitic people, be it a military leader as in 1 Samuel 29:4, 2 Samuel 19:22, 1 Kings 5:4 and 1 Kings 11:14, or a legal adversary as in Psalms 109:6. In Numbers 22:32 Satan is the name given to an angel who opposes Balaam's ill-advised journey and in Chronicles he is blamed for leading King David astray. But nowhere in the Old Testament is Satan described as being God's adversary. Quite the opposite, in fact. In the Book of Isaiah it is explicitly stated that the Hebrew God, Yahweh (Jehovah), is the omnipotent ruler of the universe and that he alone presides over mankind.

'I form the light and create darkness; I create peace and make Evil; I the Lord do all these things.'

Ambiguous and obscure allusions to the devil were only found in the Old Testament in retrospect.

It is thought that the notion of Satan as an adversary of God filtered into Judaic mythology during the third and second centuries CE, as a consequence of the Persian concept of dualism. Dualism held sway in the East during the millennia before Christianity because it solved the dilemma of how God could support one particular group and yet be on the side of its opponents. Dualistic thinking decreed that there was not one God but two, one benevolent and one demonic. The evil deity was always on the side of your enemy so the devil, it could be said, was always someone else's God. This was the origin of the hierarchy of hell, a list of demons and their functions that appeared in early magical texts such as *The Testament of Solomon*, which dates from the first century CE, and later treatises on black magic such as the *Pseudomonarchia Daemonum* by the 16th-century occultist Johann Wier.

In all of these books the evil spirits were named after ancient deities whose worshippers had been conquered and their Gods demonized. Beelzebub, 'the prince of devils', had been Baalzebub, god of the Philistines, Ashtaroth was the dark goddess of the Phoenicians and Baal was the bloodthirsty deity to whom the Canaanites sacrificed burnt offerings, namely children. Other maleficent entities were created in an effort to explain the existence of various illnesses. Mammon was the exception. The god of avarice came into being only because the words of Jesus had been misinterpreted by his followers, who thought he was referring to an evil deity when he warned them that man cannot worship both God and mammon (money).

ORIGINAL SIN

Satan appears in the company of demons in the Talmud, a collection of rabbinical commentaries on Judaic law, but the trials that he devises to tempt the pious are always at the behest of God and he often expresses his hope that the victim will prevail.

In the Book of Genesis, the serpent that tempts Eve to commit the first sin by eating the forbidden fruit is merely a snake, not Satan in disguise. That particular twist comes from Revelations 20:2 in the New Testament, thereby making the serpent's alleged crime *ex post facto* (guilty according to a law passed after the event).

Christian theologians have assumed that Satan was a synonym

for the devil in the Old Testament, but rabbinical scholars have stated that no such link was intended or should be inferred.

Satan's antecedents have been further obscured by the legend of Lucifer, the fallen angel who appears in the Apocrypha, a collection of deliberations on the meaning of the Torah. These were written by anonymous Judaic scholars, visionaries and mystics who hid their true identities behind the names of ancient rabbinical authorities in order to lend credibility to their arguments and apocalyptic legends. For this reason Orthodox Judaism disowns these texts. Nevertheless, the idea of Satan as a fallen angel persists to this day. It was Christian theologians who argued that the fallen angel in Isaiah 14:12 is in fact the figure called Satan who appears elsewhere in the Old Testament, but for Judaic scholars these mythical figures are unconnected and serve separate functions.

In the Book of Wisdom Satan is named as the bringer of death, while in the Slavonic Book of Enoch (believed to date no earlier than the first century CE) the Watcher called Satanael is identified as an evil spirit. This has compounded the belief that Satan is not an individual name but is instead a generic term for an adversary. The Book of Enoch also contains a reference to a group of satans. The angel Phanuel is heard 'fending off the satans and forbidding them to come before the Lord of spirits'.

THE SHADOW SELF

'We are each our own devil, and we make this world our hell.'
Oscar Wilde

According to the once secret teachings of Judaism, known as Kabbalah, there is a parallel universe to our own called the Kellipot, which is made up of the 'shells' or 'husks' that contain the remnants of the earlier worlds that God destroyed when he saw that they were imperfect. This is the realm over which Satan and his legion of demons now preside. But even in this cosmic scheme the Dark Spirit is said to be powerless to extinguish the divine spark that animates each of us, or to sever our connection with our Creator. Again, the idea that Satan is out to steal our souls is alien to the Judaic world view. It is yet another Christian concept grafted on by a Church that wished to set itself up as a mediator between man and his maker.

Even in his guise as Samael, the Angel of Death, Satan is not considered evil, for in Kabbalah death is a natural cosmic function that enables our immortal spirit to leave the body in order to reincarnate and so continue the work of evolution through experience. Evil is anything which seeks to counter the inexorable momentum of evolution – or the Divine Will, to use religious terminology. It is not the malign mission of one cosmic being.

But even in the multilayered world of biblical parable, that which is perfect cannot conceivably create that which is imperfect. The demonic realm must therefore be seen as an intellectual conceit of the rabbinical scholars, who have argued that everything in creation must have its opposite, just as modern physicists offer a hypothesis in order to test the validity of a theory. In Kabbalah, a shadow realm in which the divine light is excluded is a contradiction – it is yet another thread in the rich tapestry of Judaic mythology and as such not to be taken literally.

Modern Kabbalists interpret this alternative universe of the Kellipot as a symbol of our own multifaceted psyche, in which the demons personify our negative attributes and the angels represent our divine characteristics. Satan is therefore no more than our own shadow self, which manifests when we consciously indulge in evil acts or in self-delusion, while what we perceive as chaos in the world around us is merely a series of events initiated by cosmic forces as a way of testing the integrity of order in the universe.

The legend of Lucifer can be traced to a much later date. It is largely of medieval origin, being 'borrowed' from an earlier story concerning the fall of the morning star in Isaiah 14:12, with elements of Ezekiel 28 and the New Testament tale of Satan's fall in Luke 10:18. Stripped of corruption and confusion it is simply a parable on the perils of pride, for according to the Kabbalah we are all fallen angels, the light bearers who are tempted to forgo spiritual development for the lure of temporal power, the accumulation of possessions and the pursuit of pleasure.

Interestingly, the Bahá'í Faith acknowledges the existence of Satan but makes it clear that he represents our lower nature, or ego.

CHRISTIANITY

In the New Testament, Satan the tempter is recast as the Evil One, the merciless host of hell where the souls of the damned burn for all eternity if they do not repent of their sins and accept Jesus as their saviour. However, Jesus never claimed to be able to save man from original sin. The doctrine of vicarious atonement was an invention of St Paul.

It was not until the 13th century that the name of the devil came into common use. The name derives from the Greek word '*diabolos*', meaning slanderer, which was adopted when the Old Testament was translated from Aramaic. Then from *diabolos* came the Old English word 'deofol', which eventually became 'devel'.

Whatever his origins, the irony is that the devil was the best marketing strategy the Church could have created. In the Dark Ages,

Dante and Virgil in Hell, 1850.

and even today in certain devout religious sects, the threat of eternal torment was sufficient to keep the faithful on the straight and narrow, and ensure that the Church never lacked for donations.

The early Christians faced a fierce fight on two fronts as they struggled to establish their new order. As an essentially pacifist movement they rejected violence as a means of overthrowing their Roman oppressors. Instead, they used persuasion as a tool for converting the unbelievers and putting an end to persecution. But Jesus' pacifist message of brotherly love was not likely to soften the hearts of the cruel and debauched Roman emperors, who believed themselves to be Gods incarnate, nor would it convince ordinary Roman citizens to abandon their faith in the pantheon of gods they had been worshipping for generations. The promise of eternal life in paradise and the blessings of an omnipotent, benign being were not a sufficiently attractive incentive for the materialistic populace, so the Christian fathers invoked an almighty, imaginary deity – the devil. He was designed to frighten followers of 'the old religion' into adopting an itinerant Jewish mystic as their messiah, after abandoning their pagan practices.

As a recruiting agent the devil had no equal. Fear, not love, drove legions of new converts into the open arms of the Church, like a terrified child who dreads the dark. And their fevered imaginations did the rest. It was crude but highly effective propaganda.

It is a curious fact that the Romans' persecution of the early Christians had nothing to do with religious intolerance. Instead, it arose from the Christians' insistence that slaves were equal to their masters. In fact, the Romans were uncommonly tolerant of other beliefs and this is one reason why they were able to maintain law and order over their vast empire for so long.

Reading between the lines of religious allegory, however, raises the interesting possibility that some of the compilers of the Christian Gospels might have been familiar with the Kabbalistic concept of Satan as a symbol of our darker side and so did not expect their references to Satan to be taken literally. Several of Jesus' disciples, such as St Paul (born Saul of Tarsus), were of course Jews and they might have been initiates of the Essenes or the Nazarenes. These were ascetic sects who practised a form of Kabbalistic meditation known as Merkabah ('Rising In The Chariot'), which was aimed at raising the level of awareness so that the higher worlds could be perceived. If this is true, it could explain the references to Satan as 'the prince of this world' in the Book of John 12:31 and 14:30; and as 'the lord of this world' in 2 Corinthians 4:4. The writers of the Gospels seem to have been alluding to man rather than to his supernatural adversary. A closer scrutiny of the Gospels produces suspiciously few allusions to the existence of Satan and these references are left teasingly ambiguous. Matthew, for example, mentions only that he is 'the prince of demons' (Matt. 12:24) and 'the tempter' (Matt. 4:3).

But perhaps the most revealing reference to Satan in the Gospels is found in the words of Jesus himself, which were recorded in Mark 8:33 and Matthew 16:23, when he addressed Peter by that name.

'He rebuked Peter saying, "Get thee behind me Satan for thou savourest not the things that be of God, but the things that be of men".'

The meaning is clear. Peter is being admonished for his doubts by being called an adversary. And when Jesus is offered the world by Satan in Matthew 4:9, it is his own fallible human nature that is tempting him to renounce the privations and self-discipline of the spiritual path at the moment of crisis, not a supernatural villain.

THE DEVIL IS IN THE DETAIL

The bulk of Satanic lore, however, comes from the allegorical Book of Revelation, the ultimate bad trip by a religious visionary, in which Satan appears as a shape-shifter who can morph into a serpent (12:9) or a dragon (20:2) at will. But in the final apocalyptic battle he is known by another name, Apollyon (Rev. 9:11), and demoted to a mere functionary who St John predicts will be cast into a pit of fire, together with a host of defeated enemies of the Lord (20:10–15). So the New Testament is as inconsistent in naming and shaming the Evil One as its predecessor, so much so that even the Church fathers were forced to acknowledge the discrepancies. In 563CE eight bishops took part in the Council of Braga, during which they defined Satan's role as if they were creating a fictional character in a passion play, which is more or less what they were doing. They decided that Satan was not God's equal but a disgraced subordinate and they denied him any credit for the creation of the universe, which those in favour of the duality theory had lobbied for.

One would have imagined that an all-powerful deity, albeit an evil one, would not have required the sanction of a committee in order to exist and that if he did exist he would surely have taken exception to having the extent of his powers determined by mere mortals. But he failed to put in an appearance when his very existence was being questioned and no one stepped forward to point out the absurdity of the situation, so the myth of the Evil One persisted.

ISLAM

Islamic scripture talks of Shaitan, which roughly translates as 'enemy' and can refer to either a man or a spirit. In the Koran's retelling of the Genesis version of the Creation (Koran 7:11–12) the devil is named Iblis. He was a fallen angel who was punished by Allah for refusing to bow to Adam and acknowledge his divinity. Iblis considered man his inferior because man was fashioned from mud while the angels were born of fire. To anyone who has studied the esoteric tradition this is a clear analogy to the divine nature of the spirit and the temporal nature of matter. Until we reconcile these two aspects of our being we will be at war with ourselves. The exiled Iblis was given the name Shaitan, but he was allowed to roam the earth testing the moral fibre of the faithful.

Devout Muslims do not question the existence of spirits (*djin*) or the efficacy of sorcery but they have been taught that the name 'Satan' is merely a term to denote their enemies, so they frequently use it in the plural sense.

As the prophet Mohammed said in the Koran, '… they follow what the Satans recited over Solomon's kingdom. Solomon disbelieved not, but Satans disbelieved, teaching the people sorcery.' (vol. II verse 96)

SATAN AS SCAPEGOAT

So if Satan is nothing more than a myth and we are our own worst enemy, how can we account for the supposed proliferation of Satanists? The answer to that is that genuine Satanists (as opposed to those who need a Hammer Horror setting to justify their orgies) do not worship a dark deity of that name but merely assert their right to indulge their innate desires, instincts and impulses free from guilt, a philosophy that conflicts with the Judaeo-Christian concepts of morality. It is the condemnation of unrestrained sexual self-indulgence by orthodox religion and society which they see as oppressive, unnatural and the root of our neuroses. Aleister Crowley's credo 'Do what thou wilt, shall be the whole of the law,' (adopted from William Blake) is their core belief and guiding principle.

Satanists do not harbour an insane ambition to invoke the legions of hell to fight an apocalyptic battle on their behalf so that they can

Aleister Crowley took pleasure in ignoring the Ten Commandments: 'Do what thou wilt' was his credo.

dominate the world. That nightmarish scenario is entirely a creation of Christian theologians. Satanic mythology does not in fact originate with Satanists but with the early Christians, who imposed their own fears and prejudices upon an indefinable group of unbelievers in much the same way as Islamic fundamentalists have demonized the 'infidels' to justify their extremist beliefs.

Evidently, we have a need to believe in the existence of evil because it absolves us of the responsibility for our actions. Unable, or unwilling, to acknowledge our failings and those of our fellow human beings we created a scapegoat, or bogeyman, to take the blame, a figure who is conveniently invisible and so cannot be exposed as anything more substantial than a shadow. The pagans did likewise with the straw man that they ceremonially burnt at the Summer Solstice, in order to banish evil from their village. But they freely acknowledged that the figure was purely symbolic. Unfortunately, the Christian devil proved more persistent and has been behind some of the most heinous crimes ever committed. Critics of the Church say that it should consider its own role in perverting its founder's teachings before condemning its opponents as the followers of the Antichrist.

That said, many of the personalities who have been examined in this book – from Aleister Crowley and Adolf Hitler to Anton LaVey and the numerous alleged Satanically-inspired serial killers of recent years – claimed that some form of malevolent force could be summoned forth to do their bidding. But did they invoke anything other than their own inner demons? And if not, is this force within or without? Can it possess us against our will, or is it waiting to be invoked by perverse rituals and bloody sacrifice?

Chapter 2

Magic and Religion

'Satan's successes are the greatest when he appears with the name of God on his lips.'
MAHATMA GANDHI

ANCIENT EVIL

Assuming that human nature has not evolved significantly since early humans first observed their environment with some degree of curiosity, it is not unreasonable to imagine that their first thought was not an appreciation of the majesty of creation but simple self-preservation. And when darkness descended we can safely assume that our distant ancestors did not pause to admire the sunset but scurried for shelter, stopping only to arm themselves with big clubs for fear of what might be lurking in the shadows.

Survival is our most fundamental impulse, not spiritual longing. Reflection, contemplation and introspection came much later with the gradual awakening of self-awareness and a nagging curiosity concerning the meaning of life. Many of us are still none the wiser on that question today and, dare I say, the vast majority of humanity is still preoccupied with basic survival and self-gratification.

Even after the founding of the first great civilizations in Sumeria and Egypt in around 4000BCE, a human being's first instinct was not to worship the Creator but to appease the dark gods of death and destruction, for the ancient world was a harsh and hostile environment. Daily life was an unrelenting battle against the wilful destructiveness of Mother Nature, not to mention the threat posed by hungry predators, rampant disease and merciless enemies on all sides. In a world of cruelty and death the dark gods held dominion over all.

It is small wonder that men's fears found expression in legends about cosmic beings who fought for supremacy in the skies and beneath the earth, creating storms, floods, famine, earthquakes and all manner of natural disasters in the process. And in an effort to explain the phenomenon of death, which was often violent and ran-

Shamans see themselves as intermediaries between the human world and the spirit world.

dom, a belief arose in the immortality of the soul and an afterlife in which the good were rewarded and evil was punished.

This nether world of souls and shadows varied from civilization to civilization and yet all of the cultures, even the most diverse, produced strikingly similar accounts of it. But no one, we must assume, had returned from the realm of the dead to describe the soul's journey. The only conclusion one can draw is that the shamans of primitive tribes and the high priests of the earliest civilizations shared a vision of the afterlife that had been gleaned from altered states and dreams – some drug-induced and others attained through rigorous fasting and other forms of religious or magic ritual. Such altered states are of course subjective and are coloured by the individual, the limitations of their language and the culture in which their experience occurred. This accounts for the often obscure symbolism in the descriptions of the higher and lower worlds and their imaginary inhabitants, which are found in the sacred texts and images of the world's religions.

THE HORNED GOD

The earliest surviving record of a shamanic or magical ritual is a prehistoric cave painting dating from the Palaeolithic period, which is to be found in the Caverne des Trois Frères at Ariège in France. It depicts a man dressed in an animal skin, with a headdress of antlers, who appears to be engaged in some form of ritualistic dance. Some have suggested that the figure represents the Horned God of a fertility cult that survived in Europe until the Middle Ages and is the origin of the Greek god Pan. Others have proposed that it was from this source that the Christian devil acquired his hooves, horns and tail. But the painting at Ariège is of more than historical interest for it is one of the earliest examples of ritual magic. The painting was not intended to be a mere depiction of a hunting scene, for by painting their prey the shaman and his people were using the oldest magical technique known to man – they were visualizing what they desired in order to bring that event into being through their will. In short, it was mind over matter, an intuitive technique that was practised across the world and throughout the ages by cultures which had no obvious connection.

In his memoirs, *A Pattern of Islands*, British civil servant Sir Arthur Grimble, resident commissioner of the Gilbert Islands, recalled witnessing how a native shaman summoned a vast school of porpoises from the sea after sinking into a trance. The shaman emerged from his hut crying 'They come, they come!', minutes before the first porpoise was seen.

Colin Wilson, the writer, is fond of quoting the experiences of British explorer Ross Salmon as a prime example of the psychic connection between 'primitive' man and nature. In his memoirs, *My Quest For Eldorado*, Salmon described a 'trial by nature' held by the Callawaya Indians of Northern Bolivia. A young woman had been accused of being unfaithful to her husband so the elders decided to summon the tribe's sacred animal, a condor, to pass judgement on her fidelity. The condor is a reticent bird, uncommonly wary of human contact, but after the summoning ceremony three of these birds appeared, seemingly at the behest of the elders. While Salmon was filming the ceremony he caught the moment at which the huge male bird swooped down and landed in front of the terrified girl, who had been tied to a wooden post. It circled for a few moments and then ran towards her, striking its beak at her throat, before a member of the film crew chased it off with a stone. A few days later the woman committed suicide by throwing herself off a cliff. She was convinced that the bird had exposed her as a liar.

SUMERIAN MAGIC

The Horned God of the European pagans had its counterpart in the Sumerian supreme deity Marduk, who again was neither good nor evil, though he allowed evil to exist in the guise of the God Bel. In time the two deities became one – Bel-Marduk – and this new deity demanded human sacrifice. With the decline of the Sumerian empire the peoples of Babylonia and Assyria degenerated into idol worship and their magic became corrupt and self-serving. The cultural achievements of the early empire – astronomy, astrology and architecture – were abandoned in favour of blood sacrifice, superstition and conquest.

Anthropologist Ivar Lissner dates the earliest appearance of black magic to this era. The Sumerians had come up with the notion that if they could lure animals to their death by magic they might be able to defeat their human enemies by disfiguring their likeness.

At this same stage of human evolution men all around the world suddenly stopped making images in human form – all except the practitioners of what we now call the Black Arts.

EGYPT

'...the gods and magic come into existence to illuminate your majesty...'

Memorial tablet to Osiris

In earlier times the sorcerer-priests of Egypt practised dream analysis, fortune-telling, faith healing, prophecy, remote viewing, psychic surgery (operations on hypnotised patients without anaesthetic) and a form of meditation known as 'assuming the God form', which was used when someone was seeking guidance.

The person involved would sit in an attitude that was typical of the god they wished to consult – that is, as portrayed in statues and murals. Then falling into a light trance they would identify with the specific characteristics attributed to that deity, before making their appeal for assistance or guidance. It is also believed that the Egyptian high priests performed astral projection as a rite of initiation, so that they could gain first-hand experience of the secrets of life and death. However, as the priests turned from seeking insights to peddling their services they found themselves reduced to casting curses and selling safe passage through the underworld.

The priests had evolved a distinctive method of placing curses on people. First of all they fashioned a figurine bearing the name of the victim and then they fired seven stalks from seven date palms at the doll from a horse hair bow, while intoning the name of the accursed. Through such practices the high priests attained unprecedented influence and power until even the pharaoh feared offending them. It was rumoured that they could animate clay statuettes, which they would then dispatch to kill an enemy.

An account of this procedure is preserved in the Westcar Papyrus, which tells the story of a high priest, Aba-aner, who killed his wife's lover after investing a clay crocodile with life. When Pharaoh Neb-Ka visited the priest he was taken to the river bank, whereupon Aba-aner summoned the magical beast from the Nile, the body still gripped in its jaws. Impressed by the power of the priest and not wishing to incur his displeasure, the pharaoh declared 'Take that which is thine and be gone'. From that time on, the priests were immune from censure.

The temples of ancient Egypt were not places of hushed worship. Instead, they were thronged with practitioners of the magical arts, who offered visitors dream analysis, divination and guidance, all for a price. A typical appeal to the gods involved writing out a request in the blood of a bird or a small animal and then drawing an image of the god on the left hand. The hand would then be bound in consecrated cloth and the petitioner would retire to bed in the hope that the god of their choice would appear in their dreams and give them the answer they sought. To the Egyptians such practices were

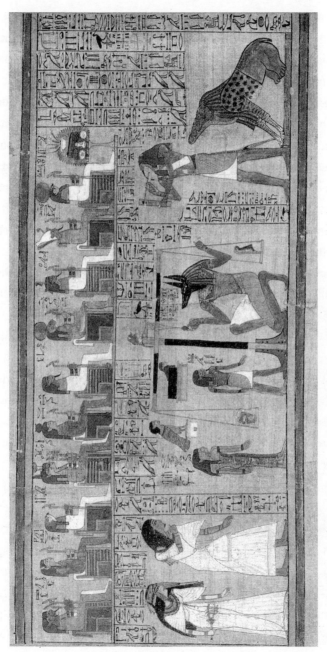

The Weighing of the Human Heart from The Book of the Dead *of Ani.*

just as harmless as consulting tarot cards or an astrologer today, but after Pharaoh Akhenaten failed to introduce monotheism (belief in one God) in 1362BCE Egypt descended into darkness. All evidence of Akhenaten's reign was erased and the priesthood became all-powerful defenders of the 'old gods'. Thereafter the cult of the dead, presided over by the jackal-headed god Anubis, dominated Egyptian society, sapping it of vitality and bringing progress to a standstill. The sun god Ammon-Ra was supplanted by Set, the evil brother of Osiris, and faith healers were superseded by magician-priests, who became increasingly preoccupied with sorcery and less so with science, thereby blurring the distinction between white and black magic.

Many sorcerers acquired bodies from the embalmers on which they practised the dark art of necromancy (communing with the dead). The embalmers were a caste of 'undesirables' who were shunned by society because they brought the stench of death with them and were said to copulate with corpses as a compensation for being forbidden to associate with women, other than the lowest prostitutes. When a beautiful young body was brought to them they would keep it fresh on a bed of warm bricks for 70 days, the prescribed period for ritual embalming, but often the temptation to preserve it beyond that time would result in putrefaction and the risk of infection. It is said that this practice might have been the origin of certain venereal diseases.

EVIL IN THE EAST

'Satan's successes are the greatest when he appears with the name of God on his lips.'

Mahatma Gandhi

A curse operates under the laws of sympathetic magic, which

state that magicians can establish a psychic link to their victim if they possess a personal object or a sample of hair or nail clippings which retain the life force of that individual. A doll made to resemble the victim will be more effective if it can be dressed in something belonging to that person. This practice is descended from the most primitive form of worship, Totenism. The Native Americans, the Inuit peoples of North America, the Arctic and Siberia and the majority of African tribes all developed from cultures centred on Totenism – the belief that the tribe's fortunes were linked to a particular species of animal.

In India this form of nature worship was contaminated by the cult of animal sacrifice, which was introduced by the Aryan tribes who invaded the Indus Valley in around 1500BCE. The central tenet of this practice is that all ills and misfortunes can be cured if they are transferred to the body of the sacred animal, which is then killed and offered to the gods. A similar notion gave rise to the symbolic expulsion of the scapegoat.

The Hindu triumvirate of gods comprises Brahma the Absolute, Vishnu and Shiva. Brahma is the creator of the universe and Vishnu is its preserver, but Shiva's role is to destroy the universe in order that it can be re-created, this time without its imperfections.

Shiva is sometimes represented as having both male and female aspects. Alternatively, he has a consort, the Mother Goddess, who can take on many forms. One of them is Kali, the multi-armed Goddess of Death. She is traditionally depicted dripping with blood, wearing a necklace of skulls and armed with a brace of lethally sharp swords. But her role, powers and significance varied according to the sect one belonged to. For the Shaktas she was to be worshipped with rituals involving orgiastic sex while the Thugees venerated her through ritual murder by strangulation. But for

Hindus all gods were simply aspects of Brahma and Kali is not seen as a destructive figure but as a symbol of change, for in Hinduism death is not an end but a phase in the endless cycle of life.

The philosophies and religions of the East all have their demons and evil spirits, but Taoism, Buddhism, Hinduism and even Zoroastrianism make no mention of the devil, for he is an exclusively Western concept.

If the devil really did exist, then surely other cultures and civilizations would at least have mentioned the fact.

DAWN OF THE MAGI

The word 'magician' derives from Magi, the name for the Persian priests of Zoroastrianism, who were skilled in the interpretation of dreams and astrology. Zoroaster (c.1700–1400BCE) was the first prophet to proclaim that the love of the Supreme Being (Ahura Mazda) was to be sought through sublimation not sacrifice and that all living creatures are of equal value to man. The fire cult was re-formed by Zoroaster, so that it became the symbol of the Universal Life Force.

According to the Gathas, a sacred text attributed to the prophet, Ahura Mazda gave birth to twin spirits who fought for control of the world. But the Supreme Being did not create good and evil, for those are human concepts. What we term good is simply the ability to perceive reality, or the truth of things, while evil is a distorted perception of the world and our purpose in it. These concepts were to have a profound, though rarely acknowledged, effect on Jewish, Christian and Muslim thought as well as on Greek philosophy.

THE GREEKS

However, it was the Greek philosophers ('lovers of wisdom') who finally dislodged the gods of the ancient world and ushered in the age of reason.

Initiation into the Greek Mysteries did not involve, as one might imagine, the sharing of wondrous secrets regarding the nature of life and death but rather the whispered admission that the gods were a fiction and that nothing was known of the afterlife. This revelation must have been a shock to the initiate, but the tactic was intentional. Having had his beliefs shattered he was then open to new ideas, specifically that the true nature of things could only be attained through deliberation and debate. It was left to the common people of Greece to worship the gods and consult the oracles.

Chapter 3

Witchcraft

The devil is only a convenient myth invented by the real malefactors of our world.'

**ROBERT ANTON WILSON
(AMERICAN SCIENCE FICTION
AUTHOR, 1932–2007)**

WITCHCRAFT IN THE CLASSICAL WORLD

The myth of the wicked witch, the caster of curses who seeks communion with the dead, is older than Christianity. In the Old Testament, King Saul is said to have consulted the Witch of Endor in order to ask the spirit of the prophet Samuel how he might defeat his enemies. Samuel responds that it is the fate of all men to surrender power to another. The witch in this tale is not evil; she is merely a medium who uses a talisman to summon the benign spirit on the king's orders, although he had expressly forbidden his subjects to dabble in the occult. It is the king who attempts to deceive her by disguising himself and flaunting his own decrees when it suits him. In the end, the witch takes pity on Saul and kills one of her own animals to feed him. The story serves only to reveal the fallibility of human nature and the dangers of hubris.

The Greeks, too, told tales of seers, sorcerers and enchantresses, for while they talked of philosophy they also consulted the oracles and practised mild forms of magic. In the *Odyssey*, the 8th century BCE poet Homer makes his titular hero summon the spirit of the seer Tiresias and encounter the enchantress Circe, neither of whom were evil. Five hundred years later witches were still a figment of the poetic imagination, for the poet Theocritus conjured up the image of a broken-hearted girl who was driven to praying to Hecate, the goddess of hell, in order to have her faithless lover back in her arms. But again, this novice witch was not evil.

Neither was Glaukias, the hero of a passage in Lucian's *Philopseudes*, which is the oldest known text to refer to the witches' love spell known as 'drawing down the moon'. Glaukias was so in love with the beautiful Chrysis that he feared that he would die of

The sorceress Circe offers Odysseus drugged wine in this painting by John William Waterhouse, 1871.

grief if he could not see her again, so he consulted a magician who invoked Hecate, the goddess of the dead. Glaukias was instructed to fashion a clay image of his beloved and stick bronze needles into it, while repeating the words, 'I pierce thee that thou should'st think of me'. The spell proved successful, for Chrysis ran to the lovesick youth and threw her arms around him, swearing undying affection. Lucian's fable suggests that although the radical thinkers of Greek society were advancing the concept of free will and consigning the gods to their poetic past, they were still chained to the idea that one individual could influence another by exercising their superior willpower.

ROMANS

It was the Roman scribes Horace, Ovid, Petronius, Lucan and Apuleius who created the iconic image of the witch as a withered old hag who scoured graveyards for the ingredients of some noxious brew and conversed with her familiars. Lucius Apuleius made his name with the first full-length story of witchcraft, *The Golden Ass*, in the second century CE. Although it was a satire that followed the author's misadventures after he had smeared himself with a witch's ointment, there was a serious lesson to be learnt from it, which is that the Left Hand Path was fraught with danger. The wise man or woman would do well to keep to the Right Hand Path or risk making an ass of themselves.

There was no moral to be drawn from the description of a necromantic ritual in Lucan's fable *Pharsalia*, just sheer terror from the thought that such practices might be possible. In this account Sextus Pompey, son of the Roman general Pompey the Great (106–48BCE), consulted the most formidable necromancer of the classical world, Erichtho, to learn if his father would be victorious against

Caesar. Erichtho, who Lucan describes as 'foul with filthiness' and dreadful to look upon, lived in a cemetery in Thessaly and slept in a tomb surrounded by relics of the dead rifled from the surrounding graves. When Sextus approached her and asked if she could predict the future, she told him that she could only learn what he needed to know from a fresh corpse, because the spirit of the dead lingered over the body and could be persuaded to return to it. But it would have to be one which had not been gravely wounded in the mouth, throat or lungs as that would prevent the reanimated corpse from speaking. She then led him to a battlefield where they found a suitable specimen, a soldier who had been recently slain.

As Sextus wrestled with revulsion at the thought of what he was about to do, Erichtho pierced the corpse's jaw with a hook and dragged it to a nearby cave. There she brewed a noxious concoction containing menstrual blood, the spittle from a mad dog and the flesh of a hyena, which she poured into a wound above the heart in order to reanimate it. Amid a deafening rumble of thunder and the crying of wild animals she called upon the dark gods Hermes, Charon, Hecate, Prosperine and Chaos to surrender the soldier's spirit, which was then seen hovering above the lifeless body. But the spirit would not obey her summons to enter the mangled corpse until she promised to burn the body afterwards so that it could never be summoned again. Only then did the soldier's ghost re-enter the body. In the ghastly light of the moon it rose shakily to its feet and foretold the future through the corpse's lips. The body was then burnt, which released the spirit.

This episode is certainly pure fiction, but such tales were not intended to be taken as fact. They were created to preserve the faith of a people who needed to believe that the spirit survived beyond death. A simple tale of a benign ghost returning to reassure its loved ones that all was well in the world beyond would not have gripped the imagination as did the gruesome story of Erichtho.

GOSPEL OF THE WITCHES

Evidence that the cult of witchcraft was a formalized religion that predated Christianity was only unearthed in 1886, when the American folklorist Charles Leland discovered an intriguing document during a trip to Italy. He had travelled there to research gypsy customs but during his visit he met a self-confessed witch by the name of Maddalena, who produced a handwritten copy of *Aradia – Gospel of the Witches*, which dispelled the image of witchcraft as a hellish rite. There was no mention of the devil, sex with Satan or sacrifice. Instead the book outlined the belief that a universal life force resided in all living things and that this source of power could be tapped into and channelled by those who could attune themselves to it. Leland was convinced that the book was a genuine artefact and that it had been passed down to Maddalena as part of her initiation into *La Vecchia Religione* (The Old Religion) – a term that is often applied to Italian witchcraft.

The document offers an alternative creation myth in which Diana, the moon goddess, gives birth to Aradia, goddess of magic, after having been impregnated by her brother Lucifer, the sun god. There is no suggestion that Lucifer is anything other than the god of light and fire, the active or male aspect of nature and of ourselves, while Diana is the passive aspect which manifests in humans as the nurturing instinct. But the most interesting aspect of the *Gospel* is the impression given in the text that witchcraft was on the wane when the Church instigated its persecution and was seen as no more than an archaic relic of our pagan past. The monolithic stone circles that had been raised and venerated by our ancestors were left to fall into ruin, their mystical purpose and astrological significance largely forgotten.

Many sites sacred to the pagans had been built on by the Church and the land, once venerated as the womb of Mother Earth, was being cultivated and plundered without regard for the maternal being that had provided it. Pagan festivals had been gutted of their potency and significance by being reimagined as communal celebrations of the seasons. The fertility ritual of Beltane, for example, had been replaced by a dance round an innocuous maypole. At the Church's insistence, celebrations to mark the summer solstice and the winter equinox were condemned as Witches' Sabbats, in order to ensure that rural communities were dissuaded from reviving them. But when it appeared that the Church was intent on erasing all traces of paganism, individuals evidently took it upon themselves to preserve this tradition of 'natural wisdom' by recording their beliefs and practices in documents such as the one Leland had discovered. Christianity might have been the official religion of the West for the past 2,000 years, but clearly some only paid lip service to its beliefs.

A CYNICAL STRATEGY

As the new cult of Christianity swept across Europe in the first millennium CE, the Church eradicated the 'old religion' by assimilation. It also adopted its myths, such as the concepts of virgin birth, which had been the traditional method of endorsing prophets since the time of Zoroaster, and physical resurrection – despite the fact that no mention of these events is made in contemporary accounts of Jesus' life. The birth date of the Christian messiah, December 25, came from the Mithraic cult and the Roman feast of Saturnalia.

Even the iconic image of the 'Madonna and child' was taken from the Egyptian myth of Isis and Horus.

As a result of this wholesale revisionism, the Gnostic Gospels discovered at Qumran were condemned as heretical because they did not conform to the accounts in the canonical Gospels – that is, the first four books of the New Testament. But the canonical Gospels had been written several hundred years after the Gnostic Gospels, by scribes who had no first-hand knowledge of Jesus' teachings. This cynical strategy dates back to ancient times, when a conquering nation would adopt the god of its vanquished enemy as a minor deity in order to placate its prisoners. They would be allowed to continue to worship their god in captivity and at the same time insure themselves against the wrath of the vanquished god.

Even the divinity of Jesus was in dispute until the Council of Constantine was convened at Nicaea in 325CE, at which the controversial Arius and the theologian Athanasius argued over the interpretation of the Gospels. Arius disputed Jesus' status but he was eventually overruled by supporters of the theologian, who believed that Jesus was no mere mortal but should be worshipped as the Son of God.

The eradication of earlier forms of worship extended to the building of churches on the foundations of pagan temples, though a blind eye was turned to the activities of the builders, who sought to appease their fertility gods by placing stone phalluses under the altars. Many ancient churches also bear the stone effigies of Sheela-na-Gigs – that is, naked women exposing their sexual organs.

But while these images of the past looked down on the God-fearing congregations, Pan, the playful woodland sprite and bestower of sexual potency, was being demonized as a purveyor of sin and his followers were being condemned as the servants of an unholy master. Had the Church possessed the strength of its own convictions it might have waited patiently for the old ways to die out, but it saw its temporal authority challenged by a rural tradition which saw nothing sinful in sex. The Church retaliated by decreeing that sex would have to be sanctioned by marriage.

Satan had become a symbol of anything or anyone who opposed the authority of the Church, but in exercising its authority with such brutality while turning a blind eye to the excesses and indulgences of its own officials, it could be argued that Satan was the shadow of Christianity and that is why the zealots feared him.

As the writer Colin Wilson remarked, 'Christianity became a dark and morbid religion, obsessed with sin and evil … It is a sad comment on what had become of Jesus' religion of love and forgiveness.'

BURN, WITCH, BURN!

'It is a revenge the devil sometimes takes upon the virtuous, that he entraps them by the force of the very passion they have suppressed and think themselves superior to.'

George Santayana (Spanish-American philosopher and poet)

It is highly significant that the Church did not take the practice of witchcraft seriously until the 14th century, when Pope John XXII sanctioned a witch hunt in the belief that his enemies were plotting to murder him by magical means. His suspicions were well founded. Three bishops led by Hugh Geraud, Bishop of Cahors, admitted to testing the potency of their powers by putting a curse on a wax image of the pope's nephew.

The boy subsequently died. Buoyed by their success, they anointed images of the pope and two leading members of the papal court at Avignon and then entrusted their servants to smuggle them into the court, hidden inside loaves of bread. But the servants were searched at the entrance and the plot was uncovered. Among the incriminating items recovered were poisons, herbs, toads and the hair of a hanged man. Bishop Geraud protested his innocence but was found guilty. He was flayed alive and his body was burned.

Although the existence of witches was acknowledged by the Church prior to 1300, they were seen as harmless old women who were eking out a living by selling herbal remedies and love potions to their neighbours. The earliest Church document to mention witches, the Canon Episcopi, dates from the 4th century. It pours scorn on the belief that witches were 'abandoned women perverted by Satan' who possessed the power to fly through the air.'

In the 12th century the authority of the pope was being questioned by a puritanical sect called the Cathars ('the pure ones'), who accused the Church of corruption and its ministers of hypocrisy for enriching themselves at their parishioners' expense and abandoning the doctrine of piety and poverty that Jesus and his disciples had preached. The Cathars also believed in a universe in which God and Satan were at war, which gave the Church the opportunity to spread the rumour that they worshipped Satan in person and practised witchcraft. However, little was done until 1208, when the pope's legate was murdered by the Cathars. Incensed by this act, Pope Innocent III declared a crusade against the Cathars, or Albigensians.

The Church sanctioned the wholesale slaughter of all Cathar men, women and children throughout the Languedoc, an independent principality of southwest France where the sect had its centre, and in 1209 around 10,000 crusaders marched south to do the job. At Béziers one of the crusaders asked the papal legate if he could identify the heretics and was instead told to kill every one of the

'The Witches' Sleep' by Albert Keller, 1888; no one knows exactly how many witches were burnt in Europe.

20,000 inhabitants in the belief that 'God will look after his own'.

The Albigensian Crusade, as it was called, lasted until 1229. Many Cathars had by now disappeared but there were some remaining Cathar strongholds, so Pope Gregory IX instituted the Papal Inquisition. He sanctioned the use of torture to force confessions from those who would not freely admit to their blasphemous beliefs. Once condemned, they were to be burned at the stake so that their souls would then be free to return to a forgiving God. After the destruction of the Cathar citadel at Montségur in 1244 the surviving Cathars were scattered across Europe, but they were a spent force. All remaining traces of them quickly disappeared.

KNIGHTS TEMPLAR

In the Vatican vaults there is a faded document, mottled with age, that dates from August 1308. It is rarely removed from its glass display case except for study by scholars who have sought special permission from the curators. The Parchment of Chinon, as it is known, was kept secret in the Vatican City for almost 700 years, only being made public in 2004 after its existence had become public knowledge and pressure had been exerted on the papal authorities to reveal its contents.

The parchment grants absolution to the leading members of the Knights Templar, an order of warrior monks that had been formed in 1118, after the First Crusade. Their object was to protect Christian pilgrims who were travelling in the Holy Land. Many of these monks had been excommunicated for defying the authority of the pope and so had nothing to lose but their lives. The rigours of monastic life had turned them into formidable fighters and they were soon made wealthy by the generous donations bequeathed to them by grateful

The town of Lavaur was regarded as a stronghold of Satan and its population massacred as heretics.

crusaders, as well as by the Moslems who entrusted the Templars with their treasure, when it became known that these were honest men.

Legend has it that the Templars were also custodians of the Cathar treasure and that this included the Holy Grail, the cup that Jesus used at the Last Supper. It was also said that they were privy to a secret that could shake the foundations of the Church, namely that Jesus had survived the crucifixion to marry Mary Magdalene and father a child. The bloodline is thought by some to survive to this day, thereby creating a myth that has formed the basis of recent 'revisionist' histories such as *The Holy Blood and the Holy Grail* and Dan Brown's best-selling novel *The Da Vinci Code*. Proof of this 'royal bloodline' was believed to have been encoded in stone at various sacred sites including Solomon's Temple, which had been the Templars' base in Jerusalem, and the Rosslyn Chapel in Scotland where the remnants of the order fled after their persecution by Pope Clement V in 1307.

Betrayed by the Church

But there were even darker and more disturbing rumours surrounding the order. It was said that they were devil worshippers and sodomites who practised black magic before an idol called Baphomet, who took the form of a goat with cloven hooves and was furnished with both male and female sex organs. Baphomet was traditionally depicted seated cross-legged on a globe with a black candle burning between his horns and a pentagram inscribed on his forehead.

The Templars were also rumoured to prostrate themselves before a wooden phallus and a bejewelled skull before pledging their allegiance by kissing their brother initiates on the mouth, abdomen and anus. Such practices were undoubtedly untrue, stories dreamt up by their enemies to discredit them and give the Church grounds to dissolve the order and confiscate its vast wealth.

The existence of the Parchment of Chinon indicates that the Vatican itself had officially acknowledged that there were no grounds for these charges. According to the Parchment, the Templars were to be reinstated into the Catholic Church so that they could receive the sacraments after they had repented of their sins, which appear to have involved nothing more than homosexual acts.

But this offer of reconciliation was opposed by Philip IV of France, who was in desperate need of funds and resented having to borrow money from the Templars. He demanded that the pope charge the knights with heresy so that their property and wealth would be forfeited. And so it was that on 13 October 1307 all of the Templars in France were arrested and tortured in an effort to extract confessions. Within days 36 of them had died from their injuries. In the following month the ailing Pope Clement V issued a decree ordering all monarchs to sanction the arrest of any Templars in their kingdoms. The arrested knights refused to admit to any false charges and many went to their deaths believing that they had been betrayed by the Church they had risked their lives to protect.

In 1314 the Church claimed its last Templar victim. Jacques de Molay, Grand Master of the Knights Templar, was burned alive on an island in the Seine at sunset after recanting his earlier confession, which he had made under torture. As the executioner lit the faggots de Molay protested that the Templars were innocent victims of King Philip and his co-conspirator, the pope. And he cursed the two men who had condemned his loyal knights to their deaths. The king and the pope would join him at the throne of God within a year and answer to their maker. It was no idle threat. Within a year Clement V and Philip IV of France were both dead.

HAMMER OF THE WITCHES

'By the pricking of my thumbs, Something wicked this way comes.'

William Shakespeare, *Macbeth*

The Cathars had been mercilessly eradicated, but this did not satisfy Pope John XXII, whose papal bull of 1326 declared that witchcraft was a crime punishable by death. Inquisitors no longer had to prove heresy in order to justify their torture of suspected witches and as a result paranoia and persecution spread like a plague. Over the next 400 years unknown numbers of men and women throughout Europe were 'put to the test' with all manner of inhuman devices that even the devil himself could not have devised. Many of them made false confessions to end their suffering. And all in the name of a religion that had been founded on the principle of brotherly love, forgiveness and mercy.

Many of those who were dragged before the Inquisition had been denounced by their neighbours because they were old, ugly or outsiders. Some might have been heard talking to themselves, their cat or another animal 'familiar' – a sure sign of being in league with the devil according to their accusers. Others were 'put to the test' because they were known to use herbs and roots in natural remedies or for telling fortunes. But many were put to death simply for looking at their neighbours in the wrong way, for cursing them with 'the evil eye'. To justify their barbarity the Inquisition leaders quoted the biblical edict, 'Thou shalt not suffer a witch to live', but they were ignorant of the fact that a more accurate translation is 'thou shall not suffer poisoners to live' (according to scholar Reginald Scot, author of *Discoverie of Witchcraft*, published in 1584).

But not all of the pope's administrators approved of his methods. The archbishop of Rheims and two of his colleagues protested that witchcraft was a fantasy, which was sufficient to persuade the Parlement de Paris to order the release of all of its suspects.

Had it not been for the zeal of Pope Innocent VIII, who succeeded to the papal throne in 1484, the witch-hunting mania might have petered out before it could send more innocent souls to their maker. But Pope Innocent was a hardliner who took it upon himself to scourge the Earth of sinners and uproot the devil's seed.

The first act of his reign was to praise the efforts of the Vatican's 'dear sons' – Austrian inquisitor Heinrich Kramer and Jacob Sprengler, Dean of Cologne University – in revealing the extent of devil worship in Germany. The pope's endorsement was enough to encourage Kramer and Sprengler to embark on an exhaustive exposé of witchcraft, which was published two years later.

Copies of the *Malleus Maleficarum* (Hammer of the Witches) might have gathered dust on the shelves of ecclesiastical libraries and theological institutions had it not been for its authors' detailed descriptions of the sexual activities of Satan's servants. Graphic descriptions of the nocturnal habits of succubi and incubi, who were said to visit God-fearing Christians in their sleep, were augmented with scholarly debates on whether or not a witch had the power to steal a man's penis. The salacious subject matter, and the almost simultaneous invention of the printing press, ensured that the book became required reading in every monastery and household that could afford a copy. Unfortunately for the authors, the effect produced by the book was more secular than spiritual, leading its more sexually-repressed readers to vent their rage and frustration on countless suspected witches. Ironically, the witch hunts fuelled a resurgent interest in 'the old religion', which gathered momentum when the new Witchcraft Act was passed in 1735, repealing the bloody Act of 1604. People could no longer be hanged for witchcraft, which did not exist according to the authors of the Act. But they could be imprisoned and pilloried if they *pretended* to be witches.

SINS OF THE CLERGY

Corruption and immorality were not the sole preserve of heretics and pagans. During the Dark Ages and throughout the Renaissance the power of the papacy rivalled that of the Byzantine emperors and the kings of Europe. A succession of popes amassed great wealth and vast armies with which to enforce their authority, but their most formidable weapon was the threat of excommunication.

Intimidated by what amounted to a papal curse, Western rulers resisted the urge to criticize God's representative on earth. Even the excesses of the Borgia Pope, Alexander VI (1431–1503), did not beget censure. Alexander was known to enjoy witnessing sexual orgies at which Rome's highest-paid prostitutes were paid to couple with the Papal Guard while Lucrezia Borgia, his daughter, applauded and awarded prizes to the most adventurous couples. Such activities stained the sanctity of the papal palace and brought the Church of Rome within a communal wafer of the blasphemous rites of a Black Mass. According to the occult novelist Dennis Wheatley, an unholy trinity of the pope's predecessors had actually indulged in the Black Arts, namely Pope Leo I in the 5th century, Pope Honorius I two hundred years later and Pope Sylvester II in the 10/11th century. Honorius was evidently not ashamed of his diabolical practices, for he published a record of them as *The Grimoire of Pope Honorius*.

In 694CE the Council of Toledo condemned a number of priests who had said masses for the dead while the people they had named were still very much alive. The priests had been paid to perform the masses as a form of curse. The threat of excommunication did not eradicate the practice entirely however, for it was still being used as late as the 13th century.

In the Middle Ages some monastic orders were unsure of their true allegiances. For instance, in the 14th century the Bishop of Exeter recorded the day he caught the monks of Frithelstock Priory paying homage to a statue of Diana, goddess of the hunt, in the woods and ordered them to destroy it. And in 1329 a Carmelite friar, Pierre Recordi, received a life sentence after admitting that he had seduced several women by making wax images of them, which he had sprinkled with his own blood and spittle before burying them under the women's thresholds. These were not isolated cases.

BREATHE ON ME, BREATH OF GOD

Prior to the Reformation, itinerant friars roamed the countryside extorting food and donations from the peasantry, who were told that they would be committing a sin if they denied a 'man of God' sustenance or shelter. Strict vows of chastity were enforced with self-flagellation, hair shirts and penance, but even these drastic measures were often no match for the suppressed libidos of young monks. Generations of young clerics succumbed to a compulsion to seduce their young female parishioners by breathing on them during confession – a technique known as insufflation. So widespread was the practice that St Augustine, St Jerome and St Gregory were compelled to issue a public proclamation that condemned it as a form of sorcery.

The Cure of Peifane was burnt at the stake for seducing women in this fashion as were Father Louis Gaufridi and Pierre Girard of Aix-en-Provence. The latter case is of particular interest because the victim, a simple-minded girl called Charlotte Cadière, was so traumatized by Girard's repeated assaults that she exhibited the phenomenon of stigmata – bleeding wounds that correspond to those of the crucified Christ.

The extent to which priests were involved in Satanic rites can be seen from the fact that more than 50 priests were executed for sorcery and sacrilege during the reign of Louis XIV alone.

CARDINAL SINS

'The devil is the fear you hold within, the Luciferian aspect of your existence. Your chains, the darkness of ignorance are your prison.'

Patricia Cori

The consequence of all of this suppressed sexuality was an outbreak of religious hysteria, with lascivious clerics blaming the devil for tempting them into sin and neurotic nuns claiming demonic possession in order to explain their violent convulsions and their irrational compulsion to blaspheme. Forced to live a life of self-denial and isolation, many monks and nuns exhibited symptoms of unconscious exhibitionism while those who had taught them to regard their sexual urges as unnatural seized upon the opportunity to blame a supernatural scapegoat for their lewd behaviour.

In 1633 the nuns of Loudon came under the insidious influence of Urbain Grandier, a charismatic priest and father confessor. During his visits Grandier whipped the nuns into a frenzy of religious fervour and he soon had them renouncing their vows and vying for a place in his bed. But the conflict between their inflamed passions and their sworn oath to remain faithful to Christ proved too much for the less psychologically sound sisters. Jesus, they had been told, had died for their sins and here they were betraying their Lord and deriving pleasure from it. One after another they began to exhibit disturbing behaviour as mass hysteria quickly spread through the convent. It was as contagious as a fever. Nuns writhed voluptuously on the ground and groaned in gruff 'demonic' voices but none, significantly, exhibited any signs of paranormal powers – only sexual neurosis. It was the perfect example of a magical technique of entrancement, from which our modern word 'glamour' derives.

But it was not the seduction of his impressionable and vulnerable charges that secured Grandier's conviction in 1634, but a pact with Satan that his accusers claimed had been written in his own blood. It is one of the few surviving documents from the period, although its authorship is in doubt. Grandier was an insatiable womanizer, not a Satanist. None of his victims claimed that he had forced them to participate in a Black Mass and none witnessed anything which might have suggested that his interests were anything more than carnal. However, he was burnt at the stake all the same.

THE EVENTS AT LOUVIERS

A lesser-known but equally important case was that of the nuns at Louviers who succumbed to violent convulsions and disturbing hallucinations after years of abuse at the hands of their priests. At the centre of the allegations was a young orphan, Madeleine Bavent, who had been seduced by a Franciscan monk and had taken refuge in the convent to evade his unwanted advances. But unknown to Madeleine, the convent of St Louis and St Elizabeth at Louviers, near Rouen, was under the supervision of a lecherous old priest by the name of Father David. He ordered the nuns to attend communion with bared breasts and encouraged them to walk around naked on the pretext that it would be a sin to hide the beauty of the Lord's work – but of course that only applied to the younger, nubile Brides of Christ. Father David took a special interest in Madeleine, which she later claimed involved acts of 'gross indecency'.

Her ordeal did not end when Father David died in 1628. According to a confession she made at her trial in 1643, his successor, Father Picard, was equally licentious. Unlike his predecessor, he did not stop at 'indecent caresses' but repeatedly raped her. As a result, a miscarriage had to be induced to avoid a scandal. The convent gardens at Louviers were said to hold the graves of numerous infants who had been strangled at birth in order to avoid the institution's embarrassment. It is said that it was not the only such site within convent walls.

Picard died in 1642, whereupon his assistant Father Boulle took his place. The abuse continued. But now there were rumours of priests conducting Black Masses and blasphemous rites on holy ground and of 'possessed' nuns writhing on the floor and foaming at the mouth. Complaints were made to the bishop of Evreux, François Péricard, who was obliged to investigate. In the company of several Capuchin fathers, who had extensive experience of such matters, the bishop heard the lurid confessions of Madeleine and her fellow nuns. They were so fantastic that they could only have been concocted by the overactive imaginations of psychologically-disturbed individuals. But behind the Satanic imagery – tales of crucified infants, bloody communion wafers and rape by the devil in the form of a large black cat – there was clear evidence of systematic sexual abuse. The priests had attempted to lay the responsibility for their actions at the devil's door.

Some of the more lurid accounts, it seems, were the work of the bishop rather than the witnesses, who had willingly confessed in the vain hope of being spared further torture. A royal physician, Doctor Yvelin, who examined the nuns, later admitted that he had considered their statements to be untrue. He went on to say that their 'performances' during their exorcisms appeared to have been well rehearsed. The bishop was not willing to allow the case to be heard in a public court. If he could convince the Capuchins that it was all the devil's doing, he could have the hearing held behind closed doors and the sentences would serve as a warning to other convents. He got his way. Boulle and another priest were found guilty and were publicly burned. Even Picard was not permitted to rest in peace. His corpse was disinterred and placed on the pyre beside Boulle. Madeleine was sent to another convent, where she was subjected to harsh treatment and condemned as a witch. She attempted suicide but she survived, although she died in 1647 at the age of 40.

If the witchfinders of the 17th and 18th centuries were sincere in their desire to exorcise the spectre of devil worship in Europe they should have looked to their own instead of sowing the seeds of suspicion among the peasantry. Most of the scenes of debauchery and religious hysteria were to be found behind the convent walls, not in the English countryside. The devil, it seems, is never far away from those who fear him the most.

LA VOISIN

Louis XIV was said to be shaken by the revelations at Louviers. He was also incensed by the rumour that many ladies from his own court were dabbling in the occult, including his mistress, Françoise-

Athénaïs, marquise de Montespan – better known as Madame de Montespan. In 1676 the king ordered a thorough but discreet investigation into the activities of a society hostess named Catherine Deshayes. Known professionally as La Voisin, Deshayes was a fortune teller who was also rumoured to be a sorceress and a confidante of Madame de Montespan. The king's fears proved well-founded. When the authorities raided the home of Madame Deshayes they uncovered a Satanic temple and evidence of human sacrifice. There were charred bones in a furnace, including those of murdered children.

As soon as the discovery was made Louis ordered the investigators to keep their findings secret. They were also directed to suppress the confession of La Voisin, for fear that she might incriminate the prominent aristocrats who were said to have participated in the ritual killings. One particularly damning charge maintained that Madame de Montespan had attempted to displace the king's former mistress, Louise de la Vallière, by paying La Voisin to perform a Black Mass. Perhaps it was a coincidence, but La Voisin's Mass seems to have worked.

Montespan really did replace Louise in the king's affections, just months after the Mass had been performed.

But if the king thought that he could silence La Voisin, he was mistaken. The sorceress continued to offer her services to the bored and the wealthy, who sought frissons in the dark and dangerous world of the occult. When Madame de Montespan heard that she would be replaced by Louis' latest obsession, Madame de Maintenon, governess to the royal children and the king's future second wife, she flew to La Voisin and demanded another Black Mass – this time to curse the governess. La Voisin dutifully obliged, hiring the aged Abbé Guibourg as the master of ceremonies. But this time the intended victim possessed the stronger will. Madame de Maintenon

Abbé Guibourg, aided by La Voisin, performs a Black Mass to keep Madame de Montespan in power.

sidelined her rival with a whisper in the royal ear, demanding that the sorceress be silenced for good. La Voisin was arrested, but on this occasion her threats to expose the sordid secrets of the court were not enough to prevent her prosecution.

Marguerite, La Voisin's own daughter, testified to having assisted her mother at the Black Mass that had been performed by Abbé Guibourg. The girl described how Madame de Montespan had offered herself to the devil while the abbé had performed an indecent ritual on her naked body as she lay on a black-draped altar. In each hand she had held a black candle made of human fat supplied by the public executioner, who had been one of her many lovers. La Voisin was found guilty of practising sorcery and was burned alive in public in 1680. Madame de Montespan was much more fortunate. She not only escaped with her life but she was also given sufficient means to live in style during her long retirement.

TO KILL A KING

France was not the only country in Western Europe to witness an outbreak of witch hysteria. On 1 September 1589 King James VI of Scotland (later to be crowned King James I of England) was awaiting his future bride, Princess Anne of Denmark, who was being carried to Scotland by a vast Danish fleet. However, the ships were battered by a storm that was so violent that the admiral in command declared that it must have been caused by witchcraft. After the fleet had taken shelter in Norway, James sailed from Scotland to bring his bride home himself. The happy couple finally reached dry land in May 1690, after surviving a further tempest. James then decided that the storms had come about because his enemies were in league with the devil, so he ordered a major witch-hunt across Scotland.

This was not mere prenuptial nerves for it was common knowledge that the 5th Earl of Bothwell, one of his majesty's chief adversaries, consorted with witches. It later transpired that the storms had indeed been brewed at Bothwell's behest. A coven led by John Fane, a warlock, had performed the necessary magic. At their trial, Fane and his assistant Agnes Simpson confessed to obtaining items of the king's clothing, which they had wrapped around a wax effigy and then melted in a fire. When that failed they christened a cat with the king's name and drowned it in the sea.

Much of what we know today about witchcraft in the 16th and 17th centuries comes from the detailed confessions of Fane and Simpson, together with those of the many other unfortunate souls who were captured and tortured in what would be the largest witch-hunt in British history.

The accounts of the royal inquisition were recorded in the king's own treatise on the subject, which was published in 1580 under the title *Daemonologie*. James' book took the threat posed by witchcraft and seditious covens very seriously indeed. For that reason it failed to make any impression on his loyal subjects, unlike its rival publication *The Discovery of Witchcraft*, which proved very popular.

The latter had been produced by an educated country gentleman named Reginald Scot, a devout sceptic, who had brought together the numerous country tales that were in circulation at the time. He had done it for his readers' entertainment and to refute the trumped-up charges of James' inquisition.

A particularly choice tale concerned a sexually promiscuous young man who had consulted a witch because he had lost his sexual member and was desperate to find a replacement. She directed him to a nest in a high tree where a number of male members were stored, but she forbade him to choose the largest because it belonged to the parish priest.

Scot served up a *mélange* of similar tales of witches and curses, which ridiculed the superstitious peasantry and the Church, whom he accused of fanning the flames of irrational fear and ignorance. The popularity of his book inflamed the king, who condemned it for outselling his own and for making light of what he believed was a serious threat to the kingdom. James I was a petty, vindictive neurotic who was tormented by his sexual identity. He took considerable delight in witnessing the torture of his alleged assassins, but towards the end of his life he realized that he had committed a cardinal sin by forcing Fane and more than 70 other innocent individuals to make false confessions. He is said to have confessed that Scot was right. Witches and demons were a mere fiction and there was no truth in the accusations after all.

THE SALEM WITCH TRIALS

Fear and blind faith are a potentially devastating combination that can cause more lasting harm than any demon ever could. As the numerous witchhunts and religious persecutions over the centuries have demonstrated, our latent capacity for malicious mischief would shame the old devil himself.

Never was that fact more destructively demonstrated than in the small village of Salem, Massachusetts in 1692, where three spiteful children falsely accused their neighbours of practising witchcraft. As a result more than 200 innocent people were imprisoned and tortured and of these 22 were executed or died in prison.

The witch-hunt began in the home of the Reverend Samuel Parris, a humourless, ill-tempered and mean-spirited man who had recently returned to New England from Barbados with his 9-year-old daughter Elizabeth and their black servants. Elizabeth and her 11-year-old cousin Abigail Williams, together with a 12-year-old friend, Ann Putnam, soon fell under the spell of a maid, Tituba, who entertained them with tales of voodoo rites and spells for summoning spirits. These lurid stories, combined with the Reverend Parris' dour warnings against dabbling with the devil, gave the bored children an idea for getting attention and having a little fun at the expense of their strait-laced puritanical parents.

In January 1692 they faked convulsions, indulged in screaming fits and spoke in an unrecognizable language as if possessed. But the game got out of hand when the doctor who was summoned diagnosed Elizabeth as having been cursed. Tituba was severely beaten by the Reverend Parris, after which she 'confessed' to having bewitched the children with the assistance of her accomplices, a beggar woman named Sarah Good and a bedridden old lady, Sarah Osborne. When the three girls were brought before a magistrate they complained that they were prevented from testifying by the spirit of Sarah Good, which had left her body to torment them.

Both Osborne and Good denied practising witchcraft, but Tituba declared that other villagers were involved in the coven. Ann Putnam named one of them as Martha Cory, because she had laughed when the girl had performed her fake convulsions 'act'. No one was safe from the children's accusations. Even a minister, George Burroughs, was denounced and executed.

When they saw the power and hysteria that the girls had unleashed, other local children also claimed to have become pos-

'The Witch No. 1' by Joseph Baker: the Salem trials, which began in 1692, were based on the idea that Satan had to be behind anything bad that happened, even though the truth is that the proceedings were largely driven by human malice.

sessed, so that they too could accuse those they disliked.

One man was tortured to death rather than confess to being a member of the coven, because he was afraid he would forfeit his property and goods if he did so. His wife was later hanged for being a witch.

The Voice of Reason

When people farther afield learned how effectively evil was being rooted out in Salem, the girls were invited to identify suspected witches in the surrounding towns. But the magistrate at Andover refused to prosecute his neighbours on the word of a few children, so he and his family were driven out by an angry mob, who accused them of protecting a witch.

By October 1692 reason began to prevail when Increase Mather, the president of Harvard College, and Sir William Phips, the governor of Massachusetts, made a stand against the mass hysteria that surrounded them. Phips had faced hatchet-wielding savages in the past, so he was not going to be intimidated by a group of neurotic children and their fanatical supporters. He decreed that 'spectral evidence' was inadmissible in future trials and then he ordered the release of dozens of prisoners who were awaiting trial on false charges of witchcraft. By now the list of detainees included several members of the Church and a few highly regarded members of the community. Unfortunately, it was too late for some.

After the Reverend Parris was denounced he was forced to pack his belongings. His exit ended the witch-hunt as suddenly as it had begun. The Salem events were a shameful episode in American history, but as the so-called Satanic panic of the 1980s ably demonstrated (see pages 217–18), many had failed to learn that particular lesson and so history was destined to repeat itself.

THE HAND OF GLORY

Of all the accessories that were utilized by witches and black magicians, the most gruesome must be the Hand of Glory – the severed hand of a hanged man grasping a candle made from his own fat. It was thought to petrify anyone who saw it, which enabled the witch or sorcerer to rob a house without interference. The recipe for mummifying the hand was published as late as 1722, in a minor spell book known as *Little Albert*. It was used as recently as 1939, when a gang of poisoners in Philadelphia employed it to terrify their victims and intimidate witnesses.

MONTAGUE SUMMERS – A CURIOUS CLERIC

In 1926, at the height of the 'Jazz Age', an obscure Roman Catholic cleric experienced overnight success with a most unexpected best-seller. *The History of Witchcraft and Demonology* by the Reverend Montague Summers (1880–1948) was presented as a serious work of scholarship, replete as it was with lengthy Latin and French quotations, extensive footnotes and a comprehensive bibliography. Even so, it immediately aroused the wrath of the foremost thinkers of the time and it was equally condemned by the press. Author H.G. Wells vilified it as a catalogue of superstitious nonsense, while several national newspapers asked if its publication was a sophisticated practical joke. Summers, however, was in deadly earnest. He stated in his introduction that this was no mere antiquarian survey of quaint rural rites. Having separated fact from folklore he had been able to cut through to the 'core and enduring reality of Witchcraft and the witch cult throughout the ages' to conclude that 'there were and are organizations deliberately, nay even enthusiastically, devoted to the service of evil'.

In order to support his argument, Summers cited case after case in which witches had freely confessed to communing with the devil. He noted that many accounts were uncannily similar in substance despite the disparate nature of the cultures in which they had occurred. The romantic image of witches riding though the air astride a broomstick was dismissed as pure fantasy and those who claimed to have witnessed such scenes, such as Claudine Bauban, were discredited as being attention-seekers or people of unsound judgement like Julian Cox, who mistook a ritual country dance using broomsticks for a witches flight.

But it was not the depth of Summers' scholarship, nor the erudition of his arguments, which ensured that the book became a cause célèbre. It was his habit of lingering over the sexual details of the witches' satanic ceremonies. His barely repressed relish was combined with the righteous indignation of someone who had not been invited to the orgy. It was a feeling shared by many of his readers, who could only conclude that witchcraft was alive and well in the 20th century. Summers had single-handedly made the subject deliciously seductive.

Montague Summers was as extraordinary and complex a character as his contemporary, Aleister Crowley, with whom he was acquainted. A cherub-faced eccentric, he appeared to have stepped out of an 18th-century novel by Swift or Fielding, an impression that was compounded by his comical falsetto voice and peculiar hairstyle, which resembled a Regency wig. He habitually dressed in a cassock, a shovel hat and a black cape. In order to complete the picture he wore buckled shoes and twirled a silver-topped cane that depicted a lascivious scene from antiquity.

His ecumenical title was entirely fictitious. He had been ordained as a Church of England deacon in 1908, but he had not been officially accepted as a cleric. Perhaps this was because of his rumoured interest in Satanism or, more likely, his suspected sexual misconduct with choirboys, for which he was subsequently tried and acquitted. Whatever the truth, he then converted to Catholicism and passed himself off as a Catholic priest.

He was a known 'character' who was frequently caricatured as a Friar Tuck figure by newspaper cartoonists, who pictured him emerging from the British Museum library with a book on vampirism under his arm. But there were those who found him a somewhat sinister character.

Something for the Weekend?

The occult author Dennis Wheatley recalled being invited to Summers' Alresford home for the weekend, where he was entertained with stories of his host's struggles with the devil. One particularly memorable episode saw the would-be cleric performing an exorcism on a labourer's wife in Ireland. She was foaming at the mouth and had to be restrained while he performed the ceremony. At the height of the struggle a black mist was seen to issue from the woman's mouth. The dusky cloud then entered a leg of mutton that had been prepared for supper. When the time came to carve the meat the exhausted host and his guest were horrified to see it crawling with maggots. It is a good story, but the same events have been attributed to half a dozen occultists at various times, so it appears that Summers had no qualms about being economical with the truth. Of more significance is the fact that Wheatley and his wife were shocked to find that they shared their bedroom with a dozen giant spiders. A sure sign, it is said, of a black magician's presence!

The next morning, their host took the author into a room piled high with books. He selected a small leather-bound volume and offered to sell it to his guest for £50.

'It's just the thing for you,' said Summers. 'It's worth far more, but I'll let you have it for fifty.'

Somewhat embarrassed Wheatley declined the offer, saying that he could not afford it at that time.

'Never have I seen a man's expression change so swiftly,' Wheatley later wrote. 'From benevolent calm it suddenly became filled with demoniac fury. He threw down the book and flounced out of the room.'

To avoid further friction Wheatley sent himself a fictitious telegram and was back in London that evening.

Revered or Reviled?

The success of *The History of Witchcraft and Demonology* encouraged Summers to pen further volumes on related subjects (two explored the vampire legend and another investigated werewolves), all boasting a similar degree of scholarship and diligent research. He presented each volume as documentary evidence of the existence of such creatures and seemed to believe every word he had written. He also edited a translation of Kramer and Sprenger's 15th-century treatise, *Malleus Maleficarum* (Hammer of the Witches), and he put his name to a revised edition of Matthew Hopkins' infamous witch-hunter's handbook, *The Discovery of Witches*, as well as compiling several collections of Gothic horror stories. But it is for reawakening interest in witchcraft that he will be best remembered, revered or reviled.

'I have endeavoured to show the witch as she really was – an evil liver; a social pest and parasite; the devotee of a loathly and obscene creed; an adept at poisoning, blackmail, and other creeping crimes; a member of a powerful secret organization inimical to Church and State; a blasphemer in word and deed, swaying the villagers by terror and superstition; a charlatan and a quack sometimes; a bawd; an abortionist; the dark counsellor of lewd court ladies and adulterous gallants; a minister to vice and inconceivable corruption, battening upon the filth and foulest passions of the age.'

But it needs to be remembered that the 'Reverend' Montague Summers was not an entirely trustworthy or impartial source. Despite his professed religious zeal he was an active member of the pederastic Order of Chaeronea, whose interest in young boys was not purely philosophical or platonic, and he was also a member of the British Society for the Study of Sex Psychology, for whom he wrote an essay extolling the vices and virtues of the Marquis de Sade.

THE WITCHCRAFT REVIVAL

With his shock of white hair, goatee beard and horned eyebrows, Gerald Gardner looked like an aging satyr. He played the part, too, by professing a predilection for self-flagellation that had the Sunday newspapers salivating for salacious confessions. They speculated wildly on the scenes of wanton debauchery they imagined took place as his coven cavorted naked beneath the full moon. But behind the old mischief-maker's soiled and rather suspect exterior he had a genuine passion for practical mysticism and he can be credited with initiating the modern Wiccan revival, which is currently the fastest growing religion in America.

Gardner (1884–1964) lived in Malaya during his early years and there he indulged his passion for archaeology and anthropology, returning briefly to Britain in the 1920s to see if he could interest the Spiritualist movement in his self-made charms and 'magical instruments'. He was unsuccessful so he returned to Malaya, where he worked for the Colonial Customs Service until 1936. On his retirement he emigrated to Britain where he became involved with an occult society, the Rosicrucian Order Crotona Fellowship, who were practising a form of ceremonial magic that Gardner found fascinating but archaic. He resolved to enliven it with his own creation, based on the detailed descriptions of pagan fertility ceremonies that appeared in two highly influential but flawed works: *The Witch Cult In Western Europe* (1921) and *The God of the Witches* (1931), both by Professor Margaret Murray of University College, London. Murray had begun by assuming that the early witches had been delusional old women who had worshipped the devil, but she concluded by declaring that they were the remnants of a fertility cult which had been unjustly persecuted by the Church. Gardner approached witchcraft as an academic exercise in the first instance, tracing its roots back to the Stone Age. But he was also an eccentric exhibitionist, who wanted to be surrounded by acolytes who would willingly prostrate themselves at their master's feet and submit to his peculiar brand of discipline.

Gardner might also have taken ideas from Robert Graves' comprehensive history of paganism and magic, *The White Goddess*, and James Frazer's *Golden Bough*. Both books would have given him sufficient material for the *Book of Shadows*, his book of magic rituals and religious texts. Those who were too enamoured of their master to look more closely regarded it as entirely authentic.

CHAPTER 3

Crowley Lends a Hand

The writings of Dion Fortune inspired Gardner to write his own magical novel, *High Magic's Aid*, published in 1949, a turgid medieval romance in the style of Sir Walter Scott. He claimed that it utilized authentic magical rituals that were partly from *The Key of Solomon*, a medieval grimoire (book on magic), 'and partly from magical MSS in my possession'.

The Witchcraft Act of 1735 prevented him from openly admitting that he practised the Craft, but when the Act was repealed in 1951 Gardner saw his opportunity and exploited it. His second book, *Witchcraft Today* (1954), boasted a foreword by Margaret Murray, who was by then losing credibility because she had begun promoting increasingly eccentric theories, specifically the idea that all English monarchs were witches! However, her endorsement did the book no harm. It also found immediate favour with the general public, who were fascinated to learn that 'the old religion' was alive and well in modern Britain and that its adherents were not ashamed to practise their faith naked in the woods and even in the suburbs.

In 1946 Gardner commissioned Aleister Crowley to create new initiation ceremonies and rituals, with a view to forming his own version of the Craft, albeit one with a distinctly sado-masochistic theme. Ritual scourging and copulation were central to Gardnerian initiation rites and much of what passed for worship was little more than a theatre of the absurd. However, Gardner's coven attracted dozens of followers who were disenchanted with orthodox religion and they encouraged others to establish their own covens in England and America. Thankfully these converts have distanced themselves from the more sensational aspects of their founder's philosophy. They have matured into a sisterhood that empowers women and celebrates the feminine principle. It is not difficult to understand why Wicca is so popular at the present time. Orthodox religion offers women little more than a subservient role and Christianity holds women responsible for Original Sin.

Book of Shadows

The primary source of Gardnerian initiation rites, rituals and regulations is the *Book of Shadows*. Originally presented as a handwritten document purporting to be from the 17th century, it was in fact written by Gardner in the late 1940s or early 1950s. Only Gardner would have had the gall to draft a law stating that the high priestess must step down in favour of a younger woman if the coven desires it! The title *Book of Shadows* also refers to the personal record of magical workings that is kept by all witches.

Gardner's book is unique in that it outlines a plan of magical resistance to a Nazi invasion of Britain, an idea that was shared by Dion Fortune in *The Magical Battle of Britain*.

ALEX SANDERS – KING OF THE WITCHES

Behind the lacy chintz curtains of a modest terraced house in the English seaside resort of Bexhill-on-Sea, 60-year-old Alex Sanders, self-proclaimed 'King of the Witches', donned a golden mask and a weighty feathered headdress before summoning an Aztec fire spirit from a dimension beyond time and space. Then his assistants removed his robe, leaving this suburban shaman to dance around the front room holding a blazing flare in each hand. He was apparently possessed by the entity, which offered words of wisdom from the nether world.

'I get many strange looks,' he told the TV crew who had filmed the ritual for a documentary. 'Many people are frightened of me, that's their fault not mine.'

Alex was by then a frail old man who had difficulty in standing without assistance, but once the spirit was within him he felt that he could 'blaze a trail' for his 'people', protecting them from persecution and from the prying eyes of the tabloid press. Like many magicians and occultists, Alex was an unrepentant egotist and a habitual fantasist, who courted controversy and plagued the press to publicize his activities.

It was not only his appetite for publicity that infuriated many of his fellow Wiccans, who feared the lurid reports would incite persecution and ridicule: it was also his habit of embellishing the truth to make himself sound more interesting.

It appears that he was initiated into the Craft by a member of a Nottingham coven in the mid 1960s, but Alex always insisted that his Welsh grandmother, Mary Bibby, had performed the ceremony after he had walked in on her while she was performing a ritual.

'One evening in 1933, when I was seven, I was sent round to my grandmother's house for tea. For some reason I didn't knock at the door as I went in, and was confronted by my grandmother, naked, with her grey hair hanging down to her waist, standing in a circle drawn on the kitchen floor.'

When she had recovered from the shock of being discovered she told him to remove his clothes and join her inside the circle. Then she nicked his scrotum with a knife and declared that he was now one of them. After swearing him to secrecy, she informed him that she was a descendant of the Welsh chieftain and king of the witches Owain Glyn Dwr and that Alex would have the right to assume

Alex Sanders, the self-proclaimed 'King of the Witches', had an endless appetite for publicity.

the title in his time. But first he must familiarize himself with the rites of the 'old religion' by copying out the rituals from her own Book of Shadows.

Success at a Price

Whatever the truth might have been, Alex was a natural psychic, as were his brothers. His future wife and high priestess Maxine Sanders remembered that the family home was crowded with spirits, who had been drawn by the psychic energy generated by Alex's brothers and the regular seance that took place around the kitchen table.

'It wasn't unusual to walk into the Sanders' kitchen in broad daylight to find a full materialization seance in progress. Mrs Sanders would be carrying on with the chores regardless of the apparitions in attendance.'

Sanders' first effective curse was directed at his first wife, who left him when he was 26 years old, taking their two sons with her.

Alex cursed her with a fertility spell so that when she remarried she found herself burdened by three sets of twins.

But that was small consolation for the feeling of being rejected and deserted, so Alex pursued wealth and sex through the casting of spells.

'I made a dreadful mistake in using black magic in an attempt to bring myself money and sexual success. It worked all right – I was walking through Manchester and I was accosted by a middle-aged couple who told me that I was the exact double of their only son, who had died some years previously. They took me into their home,

fed and clothed me, and treated me as one of the family. They were extremely wealthy, and in 1952, when I asked them for a house of my own, with an allowance to run it on, they were quite happy to grant my wishes. I held parties, I bought expensive clothes, I was sexually promiscuous; but it was only after a time that I realized I had a fearful debt to pay.'

Several members of the Sanders family died prematurely from cancer and Alex's girlfriend committed suicide.

Taste for Publicity

These events dissuaded him from venturing further down the Left Hand Path. Instead he worked for a while as a healer, but he couldn't resist ridding one client of warts by transferring them to someone he didn't like. He also claimed to have cured one man of drug addiction and to have performed psychic abortions by sending the soul back to heaven. And when he could not persuade it to return it is said that he recommended an abortionist here on earth. He is credited with curing his own daughter Janice of a deformed foot, which her doctors had said could not be treated. On the instructions of his spirit guide, Alex bathed Janice's foot in olive oil and worked on it until he was able to twist it painlessly back into the right position.

In 1963, on the advice of his guardian angels and spirit guides, he took a menial job at the John Rylands Library in Manchester, where he could peruse copies of two legendary grimoires, *The Key of Solomon* and *The Book of the Sacred Magic of Abramelin the Mage*. But reading the books was not enough. He had to own them. One night he managed to smuggle them out of the library, but he was soon caught. Threatened with prosecution he promised to return them, but not before he had made a handwritten copy of the most potent rituals.

It is likely that he would have been asked to leave the library anyway, because he had attracted unwelcome attention to himself by persuading the *Manchester Evening News* to publish a front-page exposé of witchcraft. This incident also led to him being ostracized by his local coven, who considered him a liability.

But the press pestered him for more salacious titbits and he willingly obliged. By 1965 he claimed to preside over 100 covens from his Manchester home and to have created a familiar in the form of a baby, which had been born out of an act of sex magic with another male member of the coven. Alex appears to have been a genuine trance medium, but his claim to have channelled a 17th-century warlock named Nick Demdike was unproven. He was accused of taking the name from a 19th-century novel, *The Lancashire Witches*, by William Ainsworth, which featured a warlock of the same name.

Mixed Legacy

In 1969 another sensational Sunday newspaper report propelled Sanders into the spotlight and he found himself a minor celebrity on the talk show circuit, much to the chagrin of other witches. The report centred on Alex's claim to be able to raise the dead, a rite he performed with a straight face at Alderley Edge, in front of an astounded reporter. The 'corpse' was, of course, one of Alex's assistants, who lay dutifully still like an Egyptian mummy under layers of bandages until the appointed moment. The doctor who certified that the subject was dead to begin with was another of Alex's friends. As for the ritual, Alex was not willing to risk incurring the wrath of the gods by taking their names in vain, so he resisted the temptation to use a real incantation and instead read a recipe in reverse!

His antics and his craving for publicity angered many of those who sought to practise their beliefs privately and anonymously and Alex was acutely aware of the criticism levelled against him. In 1979 he made a full and sincere apology and expressed the hope that the amount of converts he had made to the Craft vastly outweighed the negative attention he had attracted.

Sanders died from lung cancer on Beltane Eve, 30 April 1988. It was his last wish that his son Victor should succeed him, but Victor wanted nothing to do with the movement and he emigrated to America.

The Alexandrian branch of witchcraft is now firmly established as an alternative to the Gardnerian tradition, but it is not as popular. This is partly due to the fact that Sanders depicted a negative image of witchcraft in the press but another reason must be Sanders' insistence that homosexuals be admitted – a rule that disrupts the male–female dynamic that is central to the workings of a coven.

DION FORTUNE – HIGH PRIESTESS OF MODERN MAGIC

'A religion without a goddess is halfway to atheism.'

Dion Fortune

The baleful gaze of Aleister Crowley, the self-appointed 'Great Beast' and dark guru of the Age of Aquarius, dominates 20th-century occultism, but someone else is far more worthy of the attention he commands.

Author and occultist Dion Fortune (1890–1946) was responsible for disseminating the theory and practice of ceremonial magic to a much wider circle than ever before. The information she dispensed had previously only been available to initiates of secret societies such as the Golden Dawn. Encoded in her novels – *The Winged Bull*, *The Sea Priestess*, *The Goat-Foot God* and others – were rites and rituals that modern Wiccans and magicians have been able to adapt and incorporate into a neo-pagan magical system based on the worship of the goddess, or the feminine principle. This was a departure from the 'old religion', in which the patriarchical figure of Pan stood paramount. Her many treatises on ritual magic and occult philosophy, including *The Cosmic Doctrine*, *The Mystical Qabalah* and *Sane Occultism*, were serialized in *The Occult Review*, a magazine that had a wide circulation in the 1930s. It would have been devoured by the likes of Gerald Gardner and Doreen Valiente, who were responsible for the modern witchcraft revival of the 1950s.

It is arguable that without Dion Fortune's contribution the modern Wiccan movement would not have flourished as it has done and the New Age movement would not have evolved into a form of nature-centred spirituality that is symbolized by Mother Earth and the Queen of Heaven.

DRAWING DOWN THE MOON

'All the gods are one god and all the goddesses are one goddess and there is one initiator.'

The core ritual in modern Wicca, known as Drawing Down The Moon, has always been credited to Gerald Gardner, self-proclaimed 'King of the Witches', and his high priestess Doreen Valiente, but it is, in fact, a variation on a rite described by Dion Fortune in her novel *The Sea Priestess*, published in 1938. A sacred circle is drawn around the priest and high priestess of the coven, enclosing them in a consecrated space marked at the four cardinal points of the compass and sanctified with the four elements: fire, air (incense), water and earth (salt). Then the high priest kneels before the high priestess, who stands before the altar holding a wand in one hand and a flail in the other, with her arms crossed in imitation of Osiris. The priest then places a kiss on her feet, knees, abdomen (womb), breast and finally her lips before addressing her as an incarnation of the Mother Goddess. She may then be inspired to address the coven as if channelling the goddess, or she may recite a passage from *The Book of Shadows*, the witches' 'bible', or another work which seems relevant at that moment. There is no mention of the devil or anything that could be construed as an affront to Christianity. Quite the opposite in fact.

'I am the gracious Goddess, who gives the gift of joy unto the heart of man. Upon earth, I give the knowledge of the spirit eternal; and beyond death, I give peace, and freedom, and reunion with those who have gone before. Nor do I demand sacrifice; for behold, I am the Mother of all living, and my love is poured out upon the earth.'

In Dion Fortune's novels the protagonist is usually a man who has suffered a psychological breakdown or other crisis. He is then rescued by an occultist who helps him to find balance and perspective through initiation into the Mysteries. A secondary theme will involve the *hieros gamos* (divine marriage) of the man with a woman he is destined to love. Through her he will find redemption and wholeness.

'When the body of a woman is made an altar for the worship of the Goddess who is all beauty and magnetic life ... then the Goddess enters the temple.'

The Sea Priestess

For the occultist all aspects of life, particularly the union of man and woman, have a symbolic significance. Life itself is a sacred ritual.

The Path to Enlightenment

Born Violet Mary Firth in Llandudno, Wales, she was raised as a Christian Scientist, but at the age of 20 she was driven to immerse herself in Eastern philosophy and magic after suffering a nervous breakdown while working as a teacher in a private girls' college. It was no ordinary nervous disorder, she later claimed, but the result of a sustained 'psychic attack' by the headmistress, who had studied yoga in India and had used her superior will to break down Violet's resistance and destroy her self-confidence.

'I entered a strong and healthy girl. I left it a mental and physical wreck,' she wrote.

When she recovered, she determined to learn all she could about the latent power of the mind, which she suspected was the source of all occult phenomena. Just prior to the First World War she enrolled at the Tavistock Clinic to study Freudian psychoanalysis, where she met her mentor, the Anglo-Irish mystic T.W.C. Moriarty, who inspired her short story collection, *The Secret of Dr Taverner*. After his death in 1923 she went on to join the Christian Mystic Lodge of the Theosophical Society.

In 1919 she was initiated into a 'daughter lodge' of the Hermetic Order of the Golden Dawn, from which she acquired a working knowledge of ceremonial magic, but by then the order was in decline. Its 'squabbling greybeards' spent more time arguing over points of procedure than a provincial parish council. During the three years she spent with the order she acquired her magical name, a contraction of *Deo Non Fortuna* ('by God, not by Chance'), and formed the opinion that modern occultists could not afford to ignore the insights offered by psychology. Magical orders such as the Golden Dawn were doomed to extinction, she argued, because their members were determined to preserve an arcane knowledge instead of developing it, just as orthodox religion had done before it.

She outlined her philosophy in *Sane Occultism*, the first of several books on the practical aspects of magic and psychic development.

'A knowledge of [occult] philosophy can give a clue to the researches of the scientist and balance the ecstasies of the mystic.'

As a trained psychologist and a practising occultist, she realized that the primary source of our modern malaise stems from a denial of our intuitive subconscious self, which the pagans personified as Pan, or Herne the Hunter's consort Aradia, the archetypal feminine self. It was Dion Fortune's opinion that unless we can reconcile the psychic and practical aspects of our personalities we will continue to be prey to mental disorders such as depression, as well as chronic stress-related ailments.

Novel Viewpoint

In Dion Fortune's novels, more so than in her magical tracts, it is made clear that realigning oneself with nature is the path to psychological integration and self-realization. Religion asks the believer to take the promise of the afterlife on trust, to submit one's life to the service of the Divine and resist temptation, whereas philosophy offers the afterlife only as a possibility and asks the individual to take responsibility for their own destiny. Only occultism reveals the true nature of the Greater Reality and our purpose within it and it empowers the individual with the ability to create that reality.

In the 1920s and 1930s it was not done to criticize religion. Any author who did so would have been pilloried in the press and could kiss their literary career goodbye, so Fortune made her views on Christianity known through the voices of her fictional portrayals. In *The Winged Bull*, she lets the central character, an erudite scholar and occultist, do the talking.

'And then came the heresy hunters and gave it (Christianity) a final curry-combing, taking infinite pains to get rid of everything that it had inherited from older faiths. And they had been like the modern miller, who refines all the vitamins out of the bread and gives half the population rickets. That was what was the matter with civilization, it had spiritual rickets because its spiritual food was too refined. Man can't get on without a dash of paganism, and for the most part, he doesn't try to.'

NIGHT OF THE WOLF

One doesn't have to be a magician to perform magic. Most people are unaware of the latent power of the mind and the harm they can cause when they allow their emotions to empower their thoughts and thereby manifest their secret desires. Fortunately, most of our idle daydreams of revenge evaporate into the ether when our foul mood passes. But when occultist Dion Fortune unwittingly unleashed a malevolent thought-form, she was psychically sensitive enough to 'see' the whole process take place.

She had been lying in bed dwelling on an injustice she had suffered from a rival occultist when she became aware of a 'curious drawing-out sensation' from her solar plexus, which in the esoteric tradition is the emotional energy centre of the etheric double or dream body. Within moments a large wolf had materialized beside her – she could feel its back pressing into her. At the time she knew nothing about elemental thought-forms, but she had stumbled upon the technique accidentally. Her thoughts had taken on the form of a wolf because she had visualized herself unleashing Fenris the Wolf-horror of the North, a creature from the Nordic myths, upon her rival. It had been an idle daydream, but her emotional turmoil, coupled with exhaustion, had put her into a state where she was able to involuntarily discharge etheric energy and give it the form of a mythical being. Although she was terrified, she kept her nerve. She ordered the creature off the bed and watched as it padded out of the room, morphing into a large dog as it did so.

That night another resident of the house complained of nightmares, in which they were pursued by wolves with shining eyes. The next day, she was much troubled with what her vengeful thought-form might do, so she consulted her spiritual mentor. He warned her that she was standing at the crossroads that divided the Left and the Right Hand Paths and he advised her to sever her emotional attachment to her rival by forgiving her. After that she must reabsorb the thought-form.

That evening she went into a trance-like state, in which she visualized the animal returning to her. After some time it materialized from the northern corner of the room, which she later learnt was traditionally associated with evil. It was now in the form of an alsatian. A thin string of ectoplasm stretched from the animal to Fortune's solar plexus. It grew thicker and more distinct as she willed the energy from the creature back into her own body. As the animal form faded and the glistening cord was drawn back inside her, she felt the desire to tear everything to pieces, but moments later it passed, leaving her soaked in perspiration. She observed that the most curious aspect of the whole episode was that during the 'lifetime' of the thought-form a genuine opportunity to avenge herself on her rival had been available, but she had refused to take advantage of it. She knew that doing so would have led her on the first step down the Left Hand Path.

VOODOO – CULT OF THE LIVING DEAD

One morning in 1936, the owners of a small farm on a winding dirt road near Port-au-Prince in Haiti noticed a native woman stumbling towards them out of the morning mist. She was dressed in a torn cotton smock and she appeared to be searching for someone. As she approached they asked her if they could help, but she did not answer. Her face was expressionless, her dead eyes were unseeing and her mouth was grimly set.

Then one of the farmers gasped as he recognized her. But that would be impossible because the girl he had known had died 29 years earlier.

The woman was given a cursory examination at the local hospital. All the indications were that she was deaf, mute and blind, yet she recoiled when the doctors tried to touch her and her head twitched from side to side like a bird, as if to catch what they were saying. The mystery was finally solved when the patient was formally identified by her brother and her husband. She was Felicia Felix-Mentor, who had been laid in her grave back in 1907. When a nurse asked what ailment she should record in the patient's admission notes, the doctor could only shrug and answer, 'Zombie'.

There are countless stories of zombies in the dark folklore of Haiti – pitiful creatures with no will of their own who exist in a state somewhere between life and death – but this was not one of them. The case of Felicia Felix-Mentor was investigated and documented by American writer Zora Hurston, a hardened sceptic who met and photographed the 'dead' girl and left convinced that this was a genuine victim of the Bokors, the voodoo sorcerers who practise black magic. It was an encounter Ms Hurston would never forget.

'The sight was dreadful. That blank face with the dead eyes. The eyelids were white all around the eyes as if they had been burned with acid. There was nothing you could say to her or get from her except by looking at her and the sight of this wreckage was too much to endure for long.'

Almost all Haitians believe that the dead can be brought back to life by sorcerers, who then use them as their mindless slaves, and that is why even the poor pay all they can afford to protect the graves of their loved ones. They buy a heavy stone sarcophagus and then inject the body with poison, or even mutilate the corpse. Those who are too poor to pay for protection will mount a vigil at the cemetery for days, until the body has decomposed so badly that it is of no use to the evil ones. Others will place a knife in the clenched fist of the corpse so that it can kill the Bokor in revenge for disturbing the sanctity of the grave.

The legend of the zombie, or jumbee, is not confined to the small Caribbean island of Haiti. The term is common to several African cultures, from which the practices and belief of voodoo originally derived. They were then uprooted and transplanted to the Caribbean, where the invocation of spirits was blended with the worship of saints and French Catholicism.

Fact and Fiction

Practitioners of modern voodoo distance themselves from the superstitions of their ancestors, which they see as the remnants of a rural tradition within which slaves attempted to protect themselves from the cruelty of their overseers. The dolls, or poppets, that are still offered for sale in the market places of Port-au-Prince are not figures to facilitate sympathetic magic, but power objects (*pwen*) that are created to carry messages between the living and the dead.

As such, they are nailed to the entrances of cemeteries.

The association of voodoo with black magic was the work of Christian missionaries, who attempted to divide their new native converts from the die-hard *Vodouisants*, whom they accused of practising witchcraft. The witchcraft allegation was a wicked fiction that had been encouraged by the white plantation owners, who feared that the male (*houngan*) and the female (*mambo*) priests could become so powerful that they could instigate a revolt amongst their slaves. Their fears were realized in 1791, when a voodoo sorcerer named Dutty Boukman summoned thousands of slaves to a midnight ceremony deep in the forest, where he performed a blood ritual. During a tremendous tropical storm, he ordered the assembled multitude to drink the warm blood of the pig he was sacrificing if they wished to be free of French colonial rule. When the storm subsided, the slaves melted back inland and overthrew their oppressors. During the following days dozens of plantations were overrun and their owners were brutally murdered. The French clung on to power for many years but the survivors lived in fear of the soulless servants of the Bokors, who were said to be immune to their bullets. By 1803 the last French plantation owner had been driven out and the independent black republic of Haiti was established.

The legend of the zombie was later sensationalized by Hollywood horror movies, but it has no basis in fact. Some explain the phenomenon by claiming that these unresponsive individuals are merely mentally retarded, while others say that they have been hexed by sorcerers, using drugs and a form of hypnotism. But the case of Felicia Felix-Mentor is there to remind the sceptic that unexplainable horrors really are possible in Haiti.

Chapter 4

The Dark Side

'A sound magician is a mighty god.'

DOCTOR FAUSTUS
(CHRISTOPHER MARLOWE)

THE BLACK ARTS

The modern magician seeks to master himself, not the universe. The power he harnesses is the latent power of the mind and the elemental spirits that he subdues are not malevolent entities but his own inner demons of doubt and self-deception. The modern magician has dispensed with the physical paraphernalia of altars, pentagrams, drapes and daggers. Instead, he achieves self-realization through his inner workings. Gone are the grimoires with which the medieval sorcerer sought to summon spirits to do his bidding and gone too are the conjurations that were designed to reveal the secrets of the universe. The modern adept knows that these abilities lie dormant within him and that all of the arcane books of forbidden lore do not contain the knowledge he can now access at will. He needs no 'hidden master' on the astral plane to awaken his powers and no 'barbarous words of invocation' to protect him from the legions of demons his forerunners feared to unleash upon the world. The sacred circle he draws is not to protect him from the forces he invokes, but to contain the energy he summons from the very essence of his being.

But it has not always been so.

Magic was once a seemingly random mixture of rudimentary science and superstition.

The Wisdom of Solomon

From the earliest times the most significant figures in the shaping of civilization were the priest-kings, who were versed in the moral laws of man and the arcane lore of the Mysteries. They were able to make the distinction between what was implied in the scriptures and what was commonly understood to be merely a set of moral laws given to man by God. The first of these and the most revered was King Solomon. His fame was universal, extending far beyond the lands of the Israelites over which he ruled. He had ascended the throne at the age of 12 after his father, King David, had died. The splendour of Solomon's palace surpassed even that of the pharaohs. His treasure houses were said to burst at the seams with gold, precious metals and gems the size of an eagle's egg while he was arrayed in robes of gold and velvet. At his command were 1,400 chariots, 40,000 chariot horses and 20,000 saddle horses. All of his drinking vessels were of gold, for silver was despised as an inferior metal. His palace, which he had named Iahar-Halibanon, the Forest of Lebanon, was 100 cubits long, 50 cubits broad and 30 cubits high, with ceilings of cedar wood. A forest of columns rose from the crystal-paved floors, but most marvellous of all was Solomon's throne. Made of ivory, it was so large that the king had to mount six steps to be seated upon it. Each step was guarded by a lion, one on each side, which would spread out their claws when he was seated. Two wooden lions were carved into the throne, which was surmounted by a pair of eagles, whose wings would shade the king from the merciless desert sun.

Yet greater still was Solomon's wisdom. He was wiser than Ethan the Ezrahite, Chalcol, Darda or the sons of Mahol. Even the kings of the neighbouring nations sent their wise men and philosophers to be instructed by the king of the Hebrews. For Solomon was learned – a rare thing among monarchs of that time. He composed 3,000 proverbs and 5,000 canticles, in which he displayed his knowledge of theology, the natural sciences and philosophy. The three realms of nature – the earth, the sky and the sea – obeyed his command, as did the spirits: celestial, terrestrial and infernal.

Solomon's Demons

According to legend the good spirits tended Solomon's gardens, sculpted statues from the quarried stone and spun his precious carpets. But there were other spirits with whom he was reputed to have had concourse. With the aid of the power invested in him by a magic ring, Solomon also commanded the obedience of demons, to whom it was said he owed his extraordinary wisdom. These demons were confined within the palace walls by the power of the ring and they ate with the rest of the household from tables of iron. No doubt these claims were made by those who were jealous of Solomon's wealth and power.

For all his wisdom Solomon had strayed on to the dark path under the baleful influence of a pharaoh's daughter, who seduced him into serving Ashtoreth, the goddess of the Sidonians and Moloch, the god of the Ammonites, with ritual sacrifice to their idols.

As he neared the end of his life Solomon prayed that his death might be concealed from the demons until they had finished writing the grimoires (books of ritual magic) that had been undertaken on his orders. And so Solomon turned his back on his unholy servants, leant upon his staff and knelt as if in prayer. And in that attitude he died while the demons worked on, unaware that his power over them was at an end. However, as they completed their task a reptile crawled from a crack in the floor and gnawed through the staff, whereupon the corpse of Solomon collapsed into dust and debris. The demons then fled, leaving the books behind, together with the power to recall them to life.

This is the legend of the origin of the grimoires that bear the king's name – the *Key of Solomon* which dates back to the 1st century CE and the Lemegeton, or Lesser Key of Solomon, which can be dated back to 1500CE, but which is undoubtedly of greater antiquity. Both books were translated into many languages and hand-copied in the centuries before the invention of the printing press. The oldest surviving copy of the *Key of Solomon* dates back to the 15th century. It is kept under lock and key in the 'forbidden' section of the British Museum.

THE *LEMEGETON*

The *Lemegeton* lists no fewer than 72 demons and their functions. All of them are described in detail as if they had been caught and catalogued by a supernatural bug hunter. It is strange to think that such creatures were considered to be as real as the inhabitants of the natural world, but it is even more bizarre to consider that they were credited with both vices and virtues.

More than half of the demons serve to teach the magician subjects such as mathematics, philosophy, astrology, astronomy, logic, languages, arts and ethics. According to the book's anonymous author, these inhabitants of the nether world can also be consulted on matters relating to the past, the present and the future. But there are also demons who can be commanded to labour as servants, locating personal objects that were thought lost or advising on the particular properties of certain herbs such as garlic, which traditionally kept evil spirits at bay. Other herbs acted as emetics, so that the magician was purged of impurities before he undertook a period of fasting, abstinence and chastity prior to an important ritual. This was crucial, because it was believed that an unclean spirit existed on a lower plane of existence than human beings, so magicians could reduce the risk of contamination or possession by raising their vibration to a higher level by purification. This is why it is thought to be dangerous to be under the influence of alcohol or drugs while dabbling in the occult.

The 63rd demon from the Lemegeton, which has the power to sow discord.

There is a strong element of wish fulfilment, of course, with certain demons being given the task of granting the secret desires of their master, be it wealth, status or personal qualities such as cunning or courage. Curiously, four demons are charged with providing entertainment to soothe the troubled spirit at the end of a hard day's conjuring. This comes in the form of music, together with natural sounds and visions. One demon is even allotted the task of pouring hot bath water, while others turn water into wine and back again. But the same demons can lay waste to entire cities, incinerate the magician's enemies or plague anyone they dislike with festering boils and other ailments. It is also in their power to create natural and man-made disasters, whether in the form of war, earthquakes, famines and floods.

The pleasures of the flesh are not neglected. No fewer than eleven spirits are entrusted with bewitching women so that their master might seduce them and one has the sole function of forcing them to strip naked. Science has certainly progressed since the age of magic, but human nature has evidently evolved more slowly.

PREPARATION

Today there are New Age shops in almost every town, where the aspiring adept can purchase robes, swords, altar cloths, chalices, candles, incense and crystal balls over the counter. Such things can even be bought by mail order, or over the Internet. But although the tools of the trade can be bought, experience and the sensitivity that is required to use them effectively and safely are not for sale. In past centuries magicians made their own wands, altars and robes, not only because they could not be bought so readily as today but because the act of making these items was in itself part of the ritual. It also tested the initiate's dedication to the Craft. Having been made by hand, the objects would be suffused with the owner's personal energy, like a battery charged and ready for use.

After the magician has cleansed himself and purified the room with incense, prayer and a purging ritual, he draws a circle clockwise around himself with chalk or charcoal. For those who prefer an inner working, the outline is drawn with the tip of the ritual sword.

But if the circle is to be visualized in the adept's imagination, he will need to sustain that image all through the ritual. A second circle is then drawn inside the first and the Names of Power are inscribed on it, using white chalk. Four small bowls of water, preferably holy water, are placed inside the rim as a barrier, together with sacred objects such as a Christian cross or phials of mercury. These items strengthen the barrier so that nothing unholy may enter. The crosses can be drawn or marked in salt. Finally, an inscription must be added within the rim, but this can vary according to the grimoire. The *Grimoire of Honorius*, for example, suggests the words '*Et Verbum caro factum est + Jesus autem + transiens per medium illorum ibat*' (And the Word was made flesh … But Jesus passing through the midst of them, went his way).

The *Lemegeton* instructs the 'magician to draw the triangle of Solomon two feet away so that the spirit can be imprisoned within it until dismissed'. The triangle contains a circle with the name of the archangel Michael written at the apex and the base ('Mi' – 'cha' – 'el') and three Words of Power on the outside ('Primeumatun' along the base, 'Anexhexeton' along the left side and 'Tetragrammaton' along the right).

The Modern Way

The modern magician is, however, more likely to follow a formula based on an inner working by Dion Fortune (see pages 87–92), who incorporated a rite of consecration and protection known as the Kabbalaistic Cross into the ritual. It is thought to have been a core practice of the Nazarenes, an ascetic sect of which Jesus is believed to have been an initiate. By encoding it in the Lord's Prayer he is said to have ensured that his disciples and followers would be protecting themselves without knowing its true meaning and purpose.

Facing east, the magician makes the sign of a cross with his fore-finger, from the middle of his forehead (traditionally the centre of the Third Eye of psychic sight) to his chest (the Heart Centre) while intoning the first line of the benediction, 'For thine is the King-dom'. Then he draws an imaginary line with his forefinger across his chest from left to right (connecting the spheres of Wisdom and Knowledge on the Tree of Life) while continuing the prayer, 'The Power and the Glory', then putting the palms of his hands together to conclude with 'Forever and Ever, Amen'. By doing so he affirms that the Kingdom of God is within him and that he asserts mastery of the four elements within and without.

He then visualizes himself holding aloft a cross-handled sword. Raising it with the point above his head he says aloud, 'In the name of God I take in hand the Sword of Power for defence against evil and aggression.' He visualizes himself growing in stature until he can look down upon the room from the rafters, whereupon he ima-gines himself drawing the outline of the circle in flames with the point of the sword.

Then beginning in the east he invokes the protection of the four archangels, Raphael, Gabriel, Michael and Uriel. 'Before me Raph-ael, behind me Gabriel, by my right hand Michael and by my left hand Uriel. And above me shines the light of the Shekinah, the liv-ing presence of God.'

In this way the magician has sealed himself within a circle of divine light and surrounded himself with the protecting angels at the four cardinal points – north, south, east and west.

Powerful Symbols

In addition he may choose to purify the circle with a rite known as the Banishing Ritual of the Lesser Pentagram, by drawing a five-pointed star with the two base points on the western side of the circle (behind him as he faces east). A black magician would inscribe the pentagram with the single point down and the two base points facing upwards. The pentagram is a powerful symbol because it represents man's dominion over all lower forms of life as well as the four elements of Fire, Water, Earth and Air, with himself as the fifth. The five points equate to the hands, the feet and the head.

Another powerful symbol is the Seal of Solomon (from which the Star of David derives). It is an interlaced double triangle, with one triangle resting on its broad base and the other with its point intersecting it to create a six-pointed star. The Seal of Solomon unites the symbols for fire and water and also symbolizes the central concept of magic, which states that the physical world is the manifestation of the spirit world, a concept encapsulated in the axiom, 'As above, so below'. It is said to have been the secret symbol with which King Solomon subdued the demons who wrote the grimoire which bears his name.

Every ritual had a particular purpose and was devised to attract a specific spirit. To ensure that the right entity appeared, it was necessary to burn the substances that were believed to attract it. Many of these were natural hallucinogenics such as hemlock, henbane, Indian hemp and opium. But whichever substance was chosen, it was always burned on a charcoal brazier, because charcoal smoke was believed to give the spirits form so that they could be more easily seen.

CORRESPONDENCES

Other rituals were thought to be governed by the planets, so it was vital to consult a table of correspondences which listed the fragrances, colours, minerals and other substances associated with a particular planet.

A ritual to evoke an attribute or spirit governed by Saturn, for example, would require a strong acrid-smelling scent such as that obtained by burning musk or mandrake, whereas a ritual associated with Mars would demand the use of hot substances such as sulphur, hellebore and dried blood.

If an animal sacrifice was made it was in the belief that the discharge of the beast's vital energy at the climax of the ritual would saturate the circle and so attract the spirit like a light in the darkness. But the act of killing a live creature would also serve to shock the magician into a heightened state of awareness.

At this point the incantation is spoken aloud, three times if necessary, each time with increasing sternness and expectation, as if calling a reluctant dog to heel. Spirits and demons were considered low grade life-forms, so it was thought necessary to train them like wild beasts.

An extract from the *Lemegeton* gives an idea of the formula.

'I conjure and command thee O spirit (name) by Him who spake and it was done by the Most Holy and Glorious Names of Adonai, El, Elohim, Elohe, Zebaoth, Elion, Escherce, Jah, Tetragrammaton, Sadai. Appear forthwith and show thyself to me, here outside this circle in fair and human shape, without horror or deformity or delay … Speak to me visibly, pleasantly, clearly and without deceit.'

Angelic spirits were summoned more respectfully and always with the provision that they should only come with the blessing of God. This also ensured that a mischievous demon did not take the opportunity to appear in the guise of an angel.

ALEISTER CROWLEY

'I have been accused of being a "black magician". No more foolish statement was ever made about me. I despise the thing to such an extent that I can hardly believe in the existence of people so debased and idiotic as to practise it.'

Aleister Crowley

Modern magicians understand that it is not the words that are important but the intention of the adept, because spells, invocations and ritual objects have no inherent power of their own. Some modern occultists create their own invocations and find them even more effective than the archaic spells, because they are personal.

Brief Encounter

Aleister Crowley had little use for archaic conjurations, preferring to create his own. One of the most effective of these was said to be the Liber Samekh for summoning a demon called Choronzon.

Crowley used this ritual in 1909, during a trip to Algiers. He was accompanied into the desert by a devoted pupil, Victor Neuburg, who assisted him in drawing the magic circle in the sand, followed by the Triangle of Solomon, as prescribed by the *Lemegeton*. Then they slit the throats of three pigeons and deposited their blood at the tip of each point of the triangle. Neuburg stayed in the circle while Crowley, attired in a black, hooded robe, knelt in the triangle and invited the demon to take possession of him, using an incantation from the *Grimoire of Honorius*. In one hand he held a topaz and it was within this stone that the demon appeared. Speaking in Crowley's voice it boasted of the plagues it had brought into the world in ancient times.

Neuburg remained in the protection of the circle but he was almost tempted to leave it when he realized that Crowley had been replaced by a beautiful, alluring woman, who now implored him to join her. But Neuburg reminded himself that this was an illusion, one of Choronzon's typical tricks. At that moment the demon showed its true face and let out a loud, mocking laugh. Then it tried another ruse. It offered to serve as Neuburg's assistant if only Neuburg would invite it into the circle, but Crowley had taught his pupil well and he refused. Choronzon then resorted to the oldest trick in the sorcerer's handbook. It assumed the form of Neuburg's master and begged for water to quench its thirst. But again Neuburg refused. He threatened the demon with all the torments of hell if it did not depart. It was not impressed. 'Thinkest thou, O fool, that there is any anger and any pain that I am not, or any hell but this my spirit?'

Choronzon unleashed a torrent of abuse and then threw sand into the circle, breaking the outline. Before Neuburg could repair it the demon was inside the circle clutching at his throat. Neuburg fought back furiously, repeating the Names of Power and stabbing the apparition with the sacred dagger. Choronzon broke off the attack and retreated to the triangle, whereupon it assumed the form of the alluring woman. Finally the vital energy of the pigeon's blood dissipated and it was drawn back into the world from which it had come, leaving Crowley disorientated and exhausted.

A 'nasty little boy'

The true face of the notorious magician Aleister Crowley is shrouded in myth and misinformation, much of it of his own making. Even his most devoted disciples have a distorted image of the man who wallowed in the title 'The Great Beast'.

Aleister Crowley summoned a demon called Choronzon in the Algerian desert in 1909.

Crowley was a master of manipulation, a shameless self-publicist who craved attention and took a perverse pleasure in shocking polite society with his boasts of drug addiction and debauchery. He relished his role as 'the wickedest man in the world' and did everything he could to enhance his reputation. Someone once described him as 'a nasty little boy who never grew up' and though that description does not take account of his considerable influence on the Western esoteric tradition, specifically practical magic, it is by all accounts a pretty accurate summation of his singularly unpleasant personality.

Crowley was born in Royal Leamington Spa near Stratford-upon-Avon on 12 October 1875. Christened Edward Alexander Crowley, he changed his name to Aleister while he was at university. His puritanical parents were affectionate and over-indulgent in raising their only child but he resented his strict, oppressive upbringing, later describing his mother as a 'brainless bigot'. His father died suddenly just as Aleister entered his teens and this had a profound effect on his development. As he became more and more wilful and provocative, his mother became increasingly passionate in her devotion to the Church. She attempted to instil in her only son the belief that sex was the devil's creation and that to submit to temptation was the first step on the road to damnation.

'Love was a challenge to Christianity,' Crowley later wrote and he determined to overcome it at the earliest opportunity.

At the age of 14 he seduced the housemaid in his mother's bed, while she was attending church. When he gleefully confessed, she accused him of being the Great Beast of the Apocalypse whose coming had been prophesied in the Book of Revelation and she sent him away to boarding school. Her reaction only compounded his belief that religious mania was a mild form of insanity.

Early Passions

Away from his mother's watchful eye he explored his bisexuality with reckless abandon, as well as his passion for writing pornographic poetry. His verses failed to make much of an impression in literary circles, where they were dismissed as decadent, derivative and morbidly sadistic. Undaunted, Crowley paid to have them published, because he could not accept that he could be anything other than brilliant at everything he attempted.

'It is a strange coincidence,' he later boasted, 'that one small county should have given England its two greatest poets – for one must not forget Shakespeare.'

His other consuming passion at the time was mountaineering, for which he was well-equipped both mentally and physically. His bear-like physique and fearless disregard for danger ensured that he excelled, although he lacked the team spirit and concern for his fellow climbers that is as critical to success in the sport as skill and strength. He once famously abandoned his climbing partners to their fate during an ascent of Kanchenjunga, when it looked as if they would prevent him from reaching the summit. He had been deposed as leader of the expedition for his 'sadistically cruel treatment of the porters' and when the other members of the party were buried in an avalanche he remained in his tent, sullen and spiteful, ignoring their cries for help.

First Steps to Power

But climbing and verse were forgotten when Crowley discovered the occult in his late teens. He consumed McGregor Mathers' *The Kabbalah Unveiled* and A.E. Waite's *The Book of Black Magic and of Pacts* in a single sitting, but stubbornly refused to acknowledge the debt his own books owed to both authors, whom he scorned as pretentious.

It was impossible for Crowley to compliment anyone, because he considered everyone his inferior, but he was excited by Mathers' idea that magic offered a means for rising above the mundane routine of everyday existence and that attainment in occult matters depended on one's intuition, not on intellect. As Crowley later recalled, success in magic depended on the ability to 'awaken one's creative genius' by not only believing that one's wish will become a reality but also visualizing it.

A childlike expectation of success, and a dogged determination to obtain what one desires at any cost, is crucial to the outcome of ceremonial magic. In every magical act the rational mind must be suspended because it limits the power of the unconscious, in much the same way as a disapproving parent can hinder the progress of a child by making them aware of the problems they might encounter. Crowley's initial success as a magician was the result of his unflinching belief in himself, a belief that later mutated into self-love, overshadowing his intuition.

He had a taste of his potential power at an early age. While he was an undergraduate at Cambridge he cursed a master who had refused to allow him to stage a bawdy play. He did it by sticking pins into a wax figure he had made. But the ritual did not go as Crowley had planned. On the night of a full moon, he convinced a number of his fellow students to join him in a field adjacent to St John's College. They were supposed to form a circle while he performed the conjuration. But at the critical moment one of the group lost his nerve and tried to wrest the doll from Crowley's grasp. The needle slipped and stuck into its foot. The next day the master fell down some steps and broke his ankle.

Dawn Battle

Crowley was initially delighted to be invited to join Mathers' fashionable occult circle, the Hermetic Order of the Golden Dawn, in 1898 – which counted several members of the Victorian establishment among its members, including the poet W.B. Yeats and several eminent authors. But he despaired when he discovered that they were as preoccupied with rank and regulation as the Freemasons.

'They were not protagonists in the spiritual warfare against restriction,' he observed, 'against the oppressors of the human soul, the blasphemers who denied the supremacy of the will of man.'

By which he was referring to institutionalized religion.

Crowley was impatient for power and he was obsessed with the notion that sex and magic were somehow linked, that the vital energy channelled during intercourse could be used in ritual magic so that one's deepest desires were brought into being. With his inherited wealth, veneer of sophistication and domineering personality, Crowley would not lack for admirers. They would submit to any humiliating act if he flattered them into believing that it could give birth to a 'magical child', a soulless thought-form that would do his bidding. Sex magic, however, was frowned upon by the 'grey beards' of the Golden Dawn who found Crowley's brazen ambition embarrassing and in decidedly bad taste. Crowley felt that he was entitled to an exalted rank within the society, but Mathers thought differently.

Their enmity intensified until, in 1904, the two men sparred in open court over the rights to the once-secret rituals that Crowley claimed had been bequeathed to him by the order's incorporeal 'Secret Chiefs'. Mathers successfully obtained an injunction that prevented his rival from publishing the material, but Crowley was a bad loser. He summoned Beelzebub and his 49 attendant demons to harass his enemy. Mathers retaliated by cursing Crowley's dogs and making his servants sick, but the psychic attack left him drained and defeated and he lost the subsequent appeal. The attendant publicity precipitated the dissolution of the order and propelled Crowley on to the pages of the Sunday tabloids, whose readers lapped up his tales of psychic tussles on the astral plane. But they were even more fascinated by his bizarre relationships and his drug addiction.

Drugs, Sex and the Serpent's Kiss

Crowley's voracious sexual appetites and sadistic streak were satisfied by a number of neurotic and impressionable women who willingly submitted to his demands, which he justified by claiming that they were part of an occult ritual. He even went to the extreme of filing his two canine teeth to a point so that he could give his adoring female disciples a 'serpent's kiss'.

He had also become addicted to mescaline, which over time drained his considerable inner strength and adversely affected his health. Had he not possessed such an indomitable will, he would have deteriorated at a far faster rate. Generous doses of heroin, opium and hashish clouded his judgement and perception as well as exacerbating his idiosyncrasies and his relationships, which were unconventional to say the least. Neurotic and masochistic women were fatally attracted to him, so he could dominate and abuse them as he wished.

On one occasion, acquaintances witnessed him kicking one of his mistresses, whom he had tied up and left to sleep on the floor of their apartment. Another time he locked his first wife in a wardrobe while he entertained a mistress in the same room. He was equally abusive to his male lovers and companions, using them and discarding them as if they were sick dogs.

Those who crossed him attested to the efficacy of his curses, which left one former acolyte in a state of nervous exhaustion for months afterwards. Crowley forged a psychic bond with his more devoted disciples, which was as difficult for them to break as an addiction to drugs or alcohol. It was widely believed in occult circles that Mathers' death in 1918 was a direct result of Crowley's curse.

The Book of the Law

By the time of the court case Crowley was still in his twenties, but he was already a larger than life figure in Bohemian circles and a magician of considerable power. However, his private life was a mess. He had befriended a promising young painter, Gerald Kelly, later to be president of the Royal Academy, and had jokingly offered to marry his new friend's emotionally unstable sister, Rose, to save her from the unwanted attentions of numerous suitors. The family were enraged to think that this fantasist might inherit their wealth and they became positively apoplectic when Crowley wed Rose the very next day and then dragged her off to Paris, announcing that from now on they were to be addressed as Prince and Princess Chioa Khan. All correspondence not appropriately addressed was to be returned unopened. The marriage revealed Crowley's infantile spite for all to see. He led Rose like a petulant child from Paris to Cairo and then on to Ceylon, exploiting her masochistic devotion to him even though he was clearly determined to humiliate her.

But then something entirely unpredictable occurred. Rose, now pregnant with their first child, revealed herself to be a medium. Whether this was true or not, at least it guaranteed that she would finally get her husband's full attention. She told him that he had offended the Egyptian god Horus but that if he followed her instructions to the letter he could invoke the deity who would dictate a radical new scripture that would bear his name. Crowley confessed that he thought the ritual was nonsensical, but it proved to be effective. Not only did Horus speak to him, presumably through Rose, but so too did Crowley's guardian angel, Aiwass. Together they dictated the entire text that was later published as *The Book of the Law*.

It was a pseudo-biblical pastiche that announced the establishment of a new religion, whose central tenet was that man is God and Aleister Crowley is his prophet.

'... take your fill and will of love as ye will, when, where and with whom ye will.'

Private Chaos

Had Crowley lived in America in the 1960s he might well have founded a profitable new cult. However, in the years before the First World War he was dismissed by the general public as just another crank in the mould of Theosophist leader Madame Blavatsky, who also claimed to channel esoteric wisdom from the spirit world. His self-centred philosophy did, however, influence a generation that emerged in the cynical 1970s and it was adopted as the core credo of the Church of Satan. His edict to leave the weak and vicious to their own fate and reject feelings of pity for those who suffer could have been taken directly from *The Satanic Bible*.

But during his lifetime the public's perception of Crowley's occultism was distorted by all of the brouhaha surrounding his chaotic private life. Rose was an unreliable muse. After their baby died of typhoid fever in Rangoon, she gave birth to a second child but proved to be an incapable mother. She turned to drink and was later committed to an asylum.

Summoning the Spirits

Meanwhile, Crowley had attained a degree of occult power which only his close friends and initiates were privileged to witness. One of them described how Crowley demonstrated his superior will by rendering one man unconscious and making another beg like a dog. On a further occasion the American writer William Seabrook was strolling with Crowley along Fifth Avenue in New York when he asked him for a demonstration of his abilities. Crowley agreed. He fell in step behind a stranger for a few moments, imitating his walk, and then he buckled at the knees, which caused the man to collapse on to the pavement.

Even while living in a rented London apartment, Crowley succeeded in summoning beings from the nether world. On one occasion he materialized a helmeted healing spirit and on another he summoned an army of demons, who marched around the room until they were dispelled by the first rays of the morning sun. But at Boleskin House, his newly-acquired estate on the shores of Loch Ness in Scotland, the spirits became so numerous that it is said he had to work with all the lights on, even in broad daylight, for the room was alive with shadows. Legend has it that the lodge keeper became possessed and attempted to murder his family, which prompted Crowley to take an unplanned trip to Mexico. There he claimed to have come close to making his own reflection disappear from the surface of a mirror, by sheer willpower. He realized that man is a god, but he lacked the humility to submit to this higher self as a true adept would do.

'Man is ignorant of the nature of his own being and powers ... Man is capable of being, and using, anything which he perceives, for everything that he perceives is in a certain sense part of his being.'

At Odds with the World

But for all his insights, Crowley could not resist pursuing the animal passions of his lower nature. For him, sex and submission were inseparable from magic and he became an avid devotee of his own religion.

In 1912 he fell foul of another occult group – the German-based Ordo Templis Orientis (OTO) – for revealing the secret of their order in his privately printed magazine, *The Equinox* – that is, that sex is the key to occult power. But this particular dispute was settled away from the public spotlight, with Crowley being granted permission to set up his own branch of the OTO in Britain.

When the Great War broke out Crowley fled to America, where he spread anti-British propaganda in order to spite the country that had failed to acknowledge his genius. There he sponged off wealthy friends and followers, having squandered his family fortune on an extravagant lifestyle which he was now not prepared to moderate, even though he lacked the means to sustain it. In 1916, he became exasperated by his contemporaries' continual refusal to grant him the magical grade of Magus, so he performed the ceremony himself, at the end of which he baptized a toad and then crucified it. By the end of the war his reluctant sponsors were infuriated by his arrogance and were tired of being taken for granted. It was time for 'the Beast' to move on.

Abbey of Thelema

Crowley knew he would not be welcomed back to Britain so he purchased a farmhouse in Cefalu, Sicily with the proceeds from a small inheritance and moved in with his new 'scarlet woman', Leah Hirsig (whom he named the Ape of Thoth), and a rival mistress, Ninette Shumway. Ninette, his former housekeeper, brought her young son as company for Crowley and Leah's two small children, but 'The Abbey of Thelema', as he renamed the house, was no place for children. Crowley decorated the walls of his studio – the Chamber of Nightmares – with his paintings of demons and the bedrooms with copulating couples. The two women were continually at each other's throats and drunken screaming fits were common. Crowley soon wearied of them. He used his influence and reputation to lure bored married women to his house, all of them eager for adulterous adventures far from home. His magical journals recorded his successes with barely repressed glee.

'MM, respectable married woman ... the girl is very weak, feminine, easily excitable and very keen, it being the first time she has committed adultery. Operation highly orgiastic and elixir (i.e. sperm) of first rate quality.'

Male visitors were also subject to their host's hypnotic powers. They jealously vied for his favours like the brainwashed members of a modern cult and freely offered to share their wives with the master. No doubt their judgement had been compromised by the copious quantities of cocaine and heroin on offer, from which their host partook freely. Like many men of strong character and will, Crowley believed that he could indulge his craving for drugs without becoming addicted. For a few of his guests Crowley's teachings were a revelation and were a liberation from a lifetime of social and sexual repression, but without self-discipline the doctrine of 'Do what thou wilt' was a formula for self-destruction. Magic is a solitary pursuit requiring rigorous self-discipline, which Crowley lacked in spades. He needed an audience, even if it was composed of vacuous socialites who were three rungs beneath his intellectual level and psychologically unstable. Unfortunately, some of his visitors were too eager to please their dark guru.

'THE WICKEDEST MAN IN THE WORLD'

During one magical ceremony a disciple, Raoul Loveday, drank the blood of a cat that had been sacrificed. He died soon afterwards. For a man who claimed to be an adept, Crowley was clearly out of control and unable to protect those who fawned at his feet. Perhaps he was merely a magnet for ill-fated, self-destructive individuals. Or was fate pulling the strings from the shadows? Loveday's wife, who had accompanied him to the island, later recalled having had a premonition of his death many years earlier. A photograph of the happy couple taken back in Oxford, England had been spoilt by what they thought at the time was a processing fault. Behind her husband there was a faint shadow of a figure holding its hands above its head – the very attitude in which Raoul had died. The episode signalled the end of Crowley's Bohemian retreat. Mussolini ordered that he be unceremoniously deported, but the incident whipped up a storm of lurid headlines. When it had all blown over, Crowley found he had acquired the nickname 'the wickedest man in the world'. He lived on it for the last 20 years of his life.

'This man Crowley is one of the most sinister figures of modern times,' *The Sunday Times* declared in an exposé published in 1922. 'He is a drug fiend, an author of vile books, the spreader of obscene practices.'

Discouraged from returning to Britain, Crowley embarked for Tunis with Leah and his 5-year-old son Dionysus, who had acquired a nicotine habit in his father's company and bragged of smoking several packets of Woodbines a day. Crowley did nothing to discourage him. He was incapable of affection and as irresponsible as ever. When Ninette gave birth to his second daughter, Anne Leah, the reluctant father drew up her natal chart and concluded,

'She is likely to develop into a fairly ordinary little whore.'

Within weeks he deserted both his family and his disciples, including a Negro boy he had initiated into his sex magic cult, and decamped for France alone. There he lived off friends until he exhausted their patience and emptied their pockets, while his family starved in Tunis, hoping in vain that Mussolini would relent and allow them to remain in Italy. It was while he was in Paris that he is said to have attempted the ritual that brought about his downfall – an invocation to Pan.

Raising Pan in Paris

A disciple had offered Crowley the use of his small private hotel on the Left Bank of Paris, together with permission to do whatever he wished. By this time Crowley had attracted a small coterie of followers, so he seized the opportunity to perform a rite that he had been planning for months, a rite that would be the pinnacle of his magical career.

He cleared a room at the top of the house and performed a banishing ritual to cleanse the atmosphere of all residual energy and any impressions from those who had used it previously. Then he retired behind closed doors with his chief acolyte, who had taken the name MacAleister (son of Aleister). The two men gave strict instructions that they were not to be disturbed under any circumstances.

It was late evening and the ceremony was expected to last until dawn. The others entertained themselves in the restaurant and awaited their leader's return, but as the evening wore on the atmosphere grew colder and the conversation was repeatedly interrupted by banging and loud shouts.

When morning came they stole upstairs and knocked gingerly on the door, but there was no answer. They tried the door handle but it was locked, so they had no choice but to break it down. Inside they found MacAleister dead and Crowley naked in a corner.

He was petrified with fear and gibbering like an imbecile. It took four months of quiet recuperation in a mental institution for the ghosts to leave him. But although he recovered his physical strength and his wits, he was never the same after Paris.

The Final Chapter

Now middle-aged, close to penury and desperate to fund an increasingly heavy drugs and alcohol habit, Crowley was reduced to selling his salacious memoirs to the highest bidder. At the end of a sojourn in Lisbon his current mistress deserted him, which shook him out of his stupor long enough to pursue her and beg for a reconciliation. But the 19-year-old German girl he had called 'The Monster' did not return to him. No one had turned their back on the Beast before, so the rejection left him reeling. In a melodramatic gesture he staged his own death by leaving a note under his monogrammed cigarette case, which he left on top of a cliff at the appropriately named Hell's Mouth.

But like a petulant child who has to be coaxed back into the limelight, he reappeared days later in time for the launch of an exhibition of his paintings.

Shortly afterwards he concocted a fake legal case against the author Nina Hamnett, who had described him as a black magician in her book *The Laughing Torso*. The whole affair had been cooked up by Crowley, who was scavenging for money. Nina was an old friend who allegedly agreed to split any proceeds from the libel action if Crowley was successful. But the case was dismissed when his friends refused to testify on his behalf. Even worse, the defence produced reams of his pornographic poetry

and regaled a stunned jury with accounts of his magical mastur-
bation rituals.

In dismissing the action the judge, Justice Swift, declared that he
had never heard such, 'dreadful, horrible, blasphemous stuff as that
which has been produced by the man who describes himself as ...
"the greatest living poet" '.

The case left Crowley bankrupt, but this had no effect on him
because he had been financially dependent on his friends and followers for years.

He spent the last years of his life in a seedy boarding house in
the English seaside town of Hastings. A frail shadow of his formidable former self, he was frightened of the dark. He died on 5
December 1947 from alcohol and drug addiction. His final words
– 'I am perplexed' – sum up a life squandered in self-indulgence
and a futile struggle against a society he considered responsible for
inhibiting the individual.

Overall Assessment

As the writer Colin Wilson observed, Crowley's insatiable appetite for recognition and adulation ensured that he failed to attain
the insight or the understanding of his contemporaries – visionaries such as H.G. Wells, W.B. Yeats and Albert Einstein. In their
own way, each of them was more of an adept than the most ne-
farious occultist of the age. Crowley exemplified the fate of the
modern 'black magician' who is seduced by his own image and
corrupted by the power he seeks to exert over his admirers and
enemies alike.

But for all his faults, Crowley possessed a formidable will,
intellect and imagination, which when combined with the desire
to succeed inspired him to produce a number of the cornerstones

of occult literature, including the genuinely impressive *Magick In Theory and Practice*. But even these serious works were 'booby trapped' with misinformation and dangerous detours for the unwary and inexperienced. (See box 'A Warning To The Curious', page 128). Crowley could not resist flaunting his knowledge and authority on the subject, even if it meant putting his self-interest before the well-being of his students. That is what makes him an important figure in the history of magic, but not a great one. He revelled in his disreputable reputation, although he vigorously protested that he was not a black magician, and he exploited those who slavishly followed him, for whom he felt nothing but loathing.

'I get fairly frantic,' he wrote, 'when I contemplate the idiocy of these louts.'

Crowley's fame was such that a number of fictional characters were based on him, though he was particularly flattered to be immortalized in Somerset Maugham's novel *The Magician* and Dennis Wheatley's occult thriller *The Devil Rides Out*. In the first he was the central character and in the second he is instantly recognizable as the colourful Satanist Morcata. But Crowley did not believe in the devil despite his declarations of devotion to the dark side, which were made for the benefit of the tabloid press. He enjoyed baiting the Fleet Street hacks and he delighted in imagining the righteous outrage that would follow when their stories were devoured at the breakfast table on the following morning.

'I simply went over to Satan's side; and to this hour I cannot tell why. But I found myself passionately eager to serve my new master ... I was not content to believe in a personal devil and serve him,

in the ordinary sense of the word. I wanted to get hold of him personally and become his chief of staff.'

Aleister Crowley

(*The Confessions of Aleister Crowley*)

'Magic doesn't work'

Crowley was neither a charlatan nor a fool. He knew that Satan was merely symbolic of the darkness within, but he lacked the humility to submit to his own higher self. He wrote a great deal about invoking his Holy Guardian Angel, but the being he channelled was his own bloated self. Crowley was simply too self-absorbed to qualify as a true adept.

Even his biographer, John Symonds, admitted that the one problem with magic is that 'it doesn't work'. It is an illusion. The theatrical trappings of ceremonial magic – the robes, the rituals, the incense and the invocations – are designed to effect a transformation of consciousness, a process psychologists call self-realization. Magic is not about paranormal parlour tricks.

Real magic involves attaining a heightened state of awareness of the inner worlds of one's own psyche so that the magician can exercise his will over his own inner demons and master his emotions. The distinction between the white magician and the black magician is that the former is devoted to the process of self-realization while the latter craves self-aggrandizement and control over others, who must submit to his superior will. Crowley confused sexual potency with spiritual development. Sex magic brought him adoration and devotion but by using his devotees for his own sexual gratification he sold himself short and deceived himself into believing that this was true power. In that sense he did come under Satan's thrall – he was a slave to temptation instead of its master.

A WARNING TO THE CURIOUS

Crowley once confessed that his magical manuals contained 'just enough chocolate in them to taste like chocolate cake'. By this he meant that he was not prepared to give away all of his secrets to everyone who cared to buy his books over the counter. It was also a warning that he had peppered the pages with dangerous diversions in order to ensure that only those who had undertaken the arduous work and study necessary to become an adept would succeed using his system. The occultist Dion Fortune considered this to be a mean, spiteful and extremely dangerous strategy.

'The formulae ... on which he works, would be considered averse and evil by occultists accustomed to the Qabalistic tradition ... no hint is given of this in the text and it is an ugly trap for the unwary student. Crowley ... gives the North as the Holy Point towards which the operator turns to invoke, instead of the East, "whence light arises", as is the classical practice. Now the North is called "the place of greatest symbolic darkness", and is only the holy point of one sect, the Yezidees, or devil worshippers ... an invocation to the North, is not going to contact what most people would consider to be desirable forces.'

Samuel Mathers, who insisted on being addressed as Macgregor Mathers, Comte de Glenstrae.

THE GOLDEN DAWN

The Hermetic Order of the Golden Dawn was not, as many authorities on the occult have suggested, a sinister Victorian secret society dedicated to the practice of forbidden arcane rites. Instead, it was a brotherhood of former Freemasons and eminent intellectuals, who were seeking contact with the powerful, invisible entities that they believed were overseeing the evolution of mankind. The order was not, however, entirely free from the colourful and unconventional characters who are naturally drawn to esoteric circles. In fact, the founder himself was an eccentric megalomaniac by the name of Samuel Liddell Mathers, the kilt-wearing son of a London clerk who insisted on being addressed as Macgregor Mathers, Comte de Glenstrae.

Mathers had his home in Paris decorated to look like an Egyptian temple, where he celebrated a form of Mass in honour of the goddess Isis. His costume on these occasions was a white flowing robe, with a leopard skin flung over his shoulder. When he was not engaged in magical ceremonies he liked to relax with an unusual variation of the game of chess for four players, in which his opponents were his wife and their guest of the evening. Mathers' team-mate was a disembodied spirit with whom he was in telepathic communication.

Mathers was a Freemason and a scholar of some repute. It was for his knowledge of archaic languages and practical magic that he was approached by a fellow Mason, Dr William Wynn Westcott, in March 1888 and invited to form a modern magical order, one that was far removed from those who still relied upon medieval grimoires.

Secret Manuscripts

Dr Westcott persuaded Mathers that their organization was to be like no other before it, because fate had put the basis of an entirely new magical system into their hands. Westcott had come into possession of a number of manuscripts containing occult symbols and instructions for rites, written in a cipher he had never seen before. All they had to do was decode them. The source of the manuscripts is unclear. One version of the story has Dr Westcott chancing upon them in a second-hand bookstall in Farringdon Street market. Other accounts suggest that he discovered them in the library of the Rosicrucian Society or that they came from the private collection owned by clairvoyant Frederick Hockley.

The only clue to their true origin is said to have been a reference to a German adept, Anna Sprengler of Nuremberg, which had been scribbled in a margin. Westcott is said to have corresponded with her in the hope of piecing together the system and drawing out further secrets. There are doubts, however, that Frau Sprengler ever existed. Some have even insinuated that the whole story had been concocted by Westcott and Mathers, who were looking to attract a higher calibre of members, people who would ensure that the organization was prominent and well-funded. If so they were successful. Well-known figures such as Bram Stoker, W.B. Yeats, William Peck the Astronomer Royal of Scotland, Arthur Machen, Sax Rohmer and Algernon Blackwood flocked to join the group.

But such figures would not have stayed and participated had they not been given genuine paranormal experiences which stimulated their curiosity and challenged their perception of reality.

Techniques

The practical exercises were based on a mixture of Eastern yoga, Christian Rosicrucian mysticism, Egyptian ceremonial magic and Judaic Kabbalah – all designed to achieve an expansion of consciousness and a heightened awareness of a Greater Reality. In practice this meant performing powerful visualization exercises such as the Middle Pillar, in which initiates stimulated the sacred energy centres of the etheric body (the spirit double or soul within every human being) to energize, heal and balance the mind, body and spirit. Rosicrucian rituals offered the means to awaken the Christ within, the Inner Teacher, by re-enacting the crucifixion and the resurrection of Jesus and guided explorations of the symbolic inner worlds of the psyche could be achieved by visualizing oneself travelling the paths and spheres of the Kabbalistic Tree of Life. Other techniques included astral projection and experiments with Tattwa symbols – simple coloured shapes on black card which were said to precipitate access to other dimensions when held against the forehead. The five major symbols – a red triangle, a yellow square, a silver horned moon, a blue circle and an indigo oval – represented the four elements of air, earth, fire and water and the realm of spirit.

Tattwa Symbols

The poet W.B. Yeats was at first doubtful that such a simple technique could produce any effect at all, but he was convinced when Mathers persuaded him to hold one of the symbols to his forehead and then close his eyes and describe what he saw. After reluctantly agreeing, Yeats was startled by an image that erupted from his subconscious, over which he had no control. It was that of a black Titan rising from a barren desert landscape, which Mathers explained was an elemental fire spirit. Even after this startling experience, Yeats remained unconvinced. He tested the cards again in private with only his subject present, so that he would not be influenced by anyone else, and he deliberately gave them the 'wrong' card

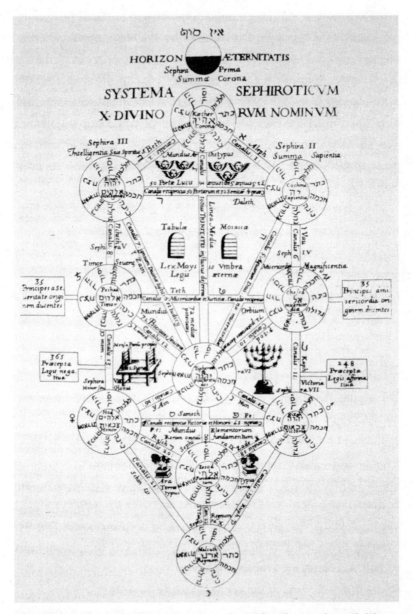

*The Sefirotic Tree, which maps out metaphysical pathways through life –
from the Kabbalah.*

while describing a different one. Yeats wanted to see if his guinea pig would 'see' the image related to the card he had described or the card they had actually been given. To his surprise they saw the image appropriate to the card they held, which suggests that the symbols relate to universal archetypes. Yeats possessed a highly developed imagination and yet his intellect could not understand how such strong images could be triggered by meditating on simple coloured shapes. But he had to acknowledge that this form of magic worked. The images, he concluded,

'... drew upon associations which are beyond the reach of the individual "subconscious" ... that the borders of our memory are (ever) shifting and that our memories are a part of one great memory, the memory of Nature herself ... and that this ... great memory can be evoked by symbols.'

Things Fall Apart

The members of the Golden Dawn considered themselves to be the custodians of an ageless wisdom, which they guarded as jealously as they did their title and grade within the Lodge. But it was their leader's pride that would prove to be their downfall. After passing the various initiation rites with incredible speed, Crowley demanded formal recognition of his achievement with the requisite rank, but his request was refused by Yeats, who disliked him intensely. Crowley appealed to Mathers, who consented, but Yeats would not be bullied. The dispute was aired in open court, which signalled the beginning of the end of the original order.

At its peak the Golden Dawn was able to claim more than 300 members, a third of whom were women, and the establishment of lodges in Edinburgh, Paris and Chicago. Today, several organizations claim direct descent from the original Golden Dawn, but they are based in the United States and New Zealand.

THEY USED DARK FORCES – NAZIS AND THE OCCULT

'If something profoundly evil does not lurk behind Germany's present tyranny, where, indeed, is evil to be found?'

Lewis Spence

(*Occult Causes of the Present War*, 1940)

In May 1945 the victorious Allies viewed the surrender of Nazi Germany as the climax to an apocalyptic battle between the forces of good and evil, the terrible last act of destruction envisaged in Richard Wagner's epic opera *Götterdämmerung* (Twilight of the Gods). The difference was that the Second World War had been played out upon the world stage and its consequences had been tragically real. More than 60 million men and women are thought to have sacrificed their lives to save the civilized world from barbarism and enslavement.

At the end of hostilities all were agreed that the Allied victory signified much more than the military defeat of a merciless dictatorship that had threatened to drag the world into a new Dark Age. Religious leaders, politicians and even some military figures spoke of evil having been vanquished and of the devil himself having been consumed by the diabolical forces he had unwittingly unleashed. But no one at that time thought such statements were more than rhetoric. However, many years later a number of sensationalist 'alternative histories' began to claim that there might have been something truly diabolical at the dark heart of the Nazi state.

Satan and the Swastika

In 1973 controversial historian Trevor Ravenscroft caused a stir with *The Spear of Destiny*, a highly imaginative account of Hitler's alleged obsession with an occult artefact of great power – the spear that pierced the side of Jesus at the site of his crucifixion. Legend had it that an army who marched behind it would be invincible (for a fuller account, see the author's *Nazis and the Occult*, Arcturus, 2008).

At around the same time author Gerald Suster published *Hitler – Black Magician* (later reprinted as *Hitler and the Age of Horus*), an exposé of crank Nazi pseudo sciences such as the Hollow Earth and World Ice theories that influenced Hitler's disastrous military strategy in Russia, as well as a number of bizarre experiments with impractical secret weapons, which diverted resources at a crucial point in the war. Another noted authority on the occult, Francis X. King, added his revelations in *Satan and the Swastika*, in which he detailed the activities of the Nazis' 'Occult Bureau'. Among other things, its operatives were charged with testing the efficacy of the psychics who claimed to be able to locate enemy shipping using a pendulum suspended over a map of the Atlantic. This branch of the *Abwehr* (defence department) was also said to have been used to locate deposed Italian dictator Benito Mussolini, so that he could be rescued by the German Special Forces. King also revealed details of *Reichsführer* Heinrich Himmler's plans to spend several million marks on building a Nazi 'Camelot' at Schloss Wewelsburg in Westphalia, for the 'Teutonic Knights' of the SS (see box). These three titles instigated an entire sub-genre of highly speculative 'histories', which centred on the assumption that members of the Nazi elite were in league with the devil or, at the very least, with his acolytes.

This fascinating, if absurd, idea was first mooted by novelist and former British military intelligence operative Dennis Wheatley in the 1930s, but back then Wheatley's black magic thrillers were thought of as lurid romances in the same vein as the universally popular Indiana Jones films, which came half a century later. But while Wheatley's books and Spielberg's films are pure fantasy, it is a matter of record that certain members of the Nazi elite did have an unhealthy obsession with the darker aspects of the occult.

HIMMLER'S BLACK KNIGHTS

Heinrich Himmler was by all accounts an unremarkable man, a petty bureaucrat with a scrawny physique who was devoid of personality and suffered from poor eyesight and chronic hypochondria. He would have been excluded from the SS had Hitler not appointed him head of the organization as a reward for his unwavering loyalty. A former poultry farmer and chauffeur, Himmler became the most feared official in the Nazi regime, with absolute power over life and death. Though he lacked any of the qualities that would make a great leader, he imagined himself presiding over a secret order of Teutonic knights in the mock medieval splendour of a German Camelot. When he saw the ruins of Schloss Wewelsburg in Westphalia in 1934 he knew he had found the 'spiritual home' of his black knights.

Legend had it that the site would witness the last battle between the Aryan people and their enemies from the east, a battle Himmler intended to win at all costs. The significance of the location was confirmed by experts in the *Ahnenerbe*, the Nazi Occult Bureau, who informed the *Reichsführer* that the castle had been built at the intersection of several ley lines. This meant that the earth's energies converged at its triangular-shaped foundations and could be utilized during magical rituals.

With Germany's fate at stake, money was no object. Hitler's indulgence ensured that no expense was spared in restoring the castle to its former glory. Its grand galleries and vaulted rooms were furnished with the finest tapestries and antiques. Within a year several million marks had been spent in reconstructing the building and decorating each suite in a style befitting a German hero.

The centrepiece of this lavish palace was the magnificent banqueting hall with its imposing Arthurian round table, around which were ranged the 12 carved wooden chairs that seated Himmler's 12 'knights'. The 12 chairs also represented the signs of the zodiac. A further chair, at the table's head, would be used by the *Reichsführer* himself. Below the Great Hall was the circular stone vault they called 'the realm of the dead', where 12 black pedestals stood around a deep shaft. This was the crypt in which the ashes of the fallen 'knights' were to be venerated by future generations.

Heinrich Himmler at Schloss Wewelsburg – he wanted it to be the Nazis' Camelot.

But Wewelsburg was more than a shrine. According to several high-ranking SS officers who visited the castle at Himmler's invitation, it also served as a private sanctuary for the *Reichsführer* and his inner circle, who conducted bizarre psychic experiments. SS *Brigadeführer* Walter Schellenberg witnessed a psychic circle in progress, whose members were attempting to project their minds into an adjacent room where a subject was being interrogated.

The object of the exercise was to focus their combined will so that the reluctant suspect would be forced into telling the truth. It is not recorded if they were successful.*

*The Schellenberg Memoirs, page 32

THE RUNES

The SS was originally intended to serve as Hitler's personal bodyguard, but it became the brutal right hand of the regime and a force answerable only to itself.

By creating the distinctive rituals, oaths and insignia, Himmler was able to instil into every member the belief that they were part of more than an elite fighting unit. Each man was to consider himself an initiate in a secret religious order, whose sacred duty was to subjugate the 'inferior races' by any means necessary. A New Order would then be established, in which the Aryan Master Race would rule like the pharaohs of old. SS members were indoctrinated with the idea that they were superior beings in an amoral universe, and so operated beyond the human concepts of good and evil.

It is doubtful whether any SS officer shared Himmler's perverse romantic vision, or saw the runes which decorated the SS banners, helmets, uniforms and armoured vehicles as anything more than the distinguishing accessories of their dark brotherhood. But for Himmler the runes had a supernatural significance. He borrowed the idea from the *Völkisch* occultists, who believed that runes were the true expression of the ancient Aryan culture.

According to Norse legend the runic 'alphabet' predated the written word and therefore each symbol embodied natural and magical forces. One particular rune was especially significant to the SS because it was bound up with the 13th-century *Volsunga Saga*, the most important of the Icelandic sagas, which formed the basis of Wagner's 'Ring' cycle. In both the saga and the Ring cycle Brynhyld (Brunhilde) persuaded Sigund (Siegfried) to carve the Tyr rune on his sword hilt to ensure victory in battle. Six centuries later this practice was adopted by the SS.

Some other runes used by the SS were

- *Hakenkreuz* (Hooked Cross), which had been the pagan symbol for Thor, the God of Thunder.
- *Sonnenrad* (Sunwheel Swastika). Adopted by the 5th SS Panzer Division, it was the ancient Norse symbol of the sun.
- 'Lightning flash' double *Sieg Rune*, which represented courage, victory, duty and physical strength. It was a modern invention and had no origin in paganism.
- *Wolfsangel* (Wolf Hook), which was adopted by the 2nd SS Panzer Division, known as *Das Reich*, and was believed to ward off danger.
- *Eif Rune*, which was embroidered on the uniforms of Hitler's personal adjutants as a symbol of devotion and loyalty.

Astrology

SS *Reichsführer* Heinrich Himmler commissioned several expeditions to Tibet and other remote regions of the world in search of occult artefacts and he was also a firm believer in astrology. In fact, he refused to make any significant decision before consulting his personal astrologer Wilhelm Wulff, who had a reputation for uncannily accurate forecasts. Wulff observed that Himmler possessed a working knowledge of astrology, but he asked 'the strangest and most infantile questions in his quest for astrological enlightenment about the military and political situation' which led Wulff to conclude that one of the most feared men in the regime was no adept but 'a mediocrity ... a pettifogging bureaucrat with scruples'.

In the summer of 1923 Wulff plotted the charts of Hitler, Göring and Ernst Röhm, the SA leader. He predicted a terrible fate for the future *Führer* and his followers. Hitler, said Wulff, was fated to be feared and to 'issue cruel and senseless orders', which would lead to his death in the spring of 1945. He would die at the hand of an assassin and a woman would play a prominent part in his death. Wulff's prediction proved correct. In April 1945 Hitler committed suicide in his Berlin bunker, with his mistress Eva Braun by his side.

Insidious Influences

Trevor Ravenscroft claimed that Hitler had been initiated into an occult brotherhood by Professor Karl Haushofer, who 'awakened Hitler to the real motives of the Luciferic Principality which possessed him so that he could become the conscious vehicle of its evil intent in the twentieth century'. But the professor's contribution to Hitler's rise to power was purely political. He introduced the dictator to the theories of geopolitics and specifically the concept of *Lebensraum* (living space), with which Hitler justified his invasion of neighbouring states. Professor Haushofer also persuaded his protégé to drop his trademark riding crop and tone down his rabble-rousing image in favour of a more statesman-like appearance. This strategy enabled Hitler to court a wider section of the electorate, which saw the Nazi Party increase its support significantly, until Hitler lost patience with the electoral system and seized power by force in 1933.

While there is no evidence that Hitler and his inner circle practised ritual magic, there is considerable evidence that they were influenced by the dark gurus of neopaganism, such as Guido von List (1848–1919), founder of Armanism, Lanz von Liebenfels (1874–1954), leader of the New Order of Templars and Houston Stewart Chamberlain (1855–1927), author of the virulently racist tracts that Hitler read voraciously in the years before the Great War. These proto-Nazi 'philosophers' promoted the myth that the German people were the descendants of a superior Aryan race who had survived the destruction of the legendary island of Atlantis. They also declared that it was Germany's destiny to assert its role as the Master Race and subvert the 'inferior' peoples, specifically the Negroes, the gypsies, the Slavs and the Jews, who were the '*Untermenschen*' or subhumans in this Wagnerian myth.

The Nazis put great faith in occult artefacts such as the Spear and the Holy Grail as well as in sacred sites where the earth's magnetic energies could be drawn upon for magical purposes.

'Satan's emissaries'

Such notions would have been familiar to Hitler, who had read Liebenfels' magazine *Ostara* and other occult publications in his youth, but it was the Aryan mythology component that appealed to his extreme nationalist world view, not the esoteric fantasies. Hitler put his faith in the blackjack and the bullet, not in mystical relics. He was all fired up for violent revolution and he had no patience with 'Völkisch mystics', whose hopelessly romantic view of a rural idyll seduced the working class into embracing National Socialism as a cultural revolution.

By subscribing to the Aryan myth the Nazis could be said to have cast themselves in the role of Satan's emissaries on earth, for they perverted science, religion and every facet of human endeavour to promote their evil ideology, which they enforced through fear, hate, lies and violence. They also indoctrinated their own people with their poisonous propaganda, until they willingly condoned the murder of the disabled and the infirm, the imprisonment and torture of their political enemies, the invasion and enslavement of neighbouring nations and global war and the genocide of innocent civilians. Had they succeeded in their ambitions to establish a New Order in Europe, the Nazis would have supplanted Christianity with a form of neopagan worship, with the swastika replacing the Christian cross.

As Hitler declared,

'One is either a German or a Christian. You cannot be both ... Our peasants have not forgotten their true religion. It still lives ... The old beliefs will be brought back to honour again ... The peasant will be told what the Church has destroyed for him: the whole secret knowledge of nature, of the divine, the shapeless, the daemonic ... We shall wash off the Christian veneer and bring out a religion peculiar to our race ... our peasantry still lives in heathen beliefs and values ... through the peasantry we shall really be able to destroy Christianity because there is in them a true religion rooted in nature and blood.'

The Dark Messiah

It was the regime's attempts to impose its demagogue on its own people, rather than its murderous campaigns abroad, that incensed the German Church and led to accusations of Satanic influences within the Reich. The British historian and occultist Lewis Spence expressed the unease felt by the German religious authorities in the years preceding the war when he wrote

'... the new pagan movement in Germany, the uncompromisingly Satanic origin of its method and intention admits of but little dispute. The replacement of the Cross by the swastika, the abrogation of the Sacrament in favour of a rite resembling that of the mysteries of Demeter, the persecution of the Christian churches and of their priests and ministers, and the replacement of the ritual, or service and hymnology by blasphemous offices and songs, the erection of a new godhead, the instruction of the young in the myths of the past instead of in the Scriptures – all this affords the clearest proof of Germany's relapse into that type of paganism which the Satanist policy and propaganda have invariably regarded as the most fitting medium for the destruction and extirpation of the Christian faith.'

Spence was in no doubt that Hitler was a modern Faust who had sold his soul to the devil and was now dedicated to carrying out his master's plan for world domination.

'The Führer *is merely the creature and instrument of forces which for centuries have been making use of this or that dictator, tyrant or other puppet notoriety to further their own arcane intentions, which, in a word, are the creation of general chaos and the final destruction of humanity.'*

Spence argued that Nazism was not initiated by Satanists but was infiltrated by the devil's disciples so that Germany could become their instrument for chaos and destruction.

'If the Prince of darkness in person had undertaken to govern that nation it is difficult to suggest how he could have borne himself otherwise than its unhappy leader has done, or with more fantastic wickedness.'

White Rose

The only group within Germany, other than the Church, that was sufficiently courageous to speak out against the regime was the anti-Nazi student organization known as the White Rose, led by Sophie Scholl and her brother Hans. They sacrificed themselves in a vain effort to awaken the conscience of their countrymen and expose the true nature of the enemy within.

'Every word that comes from Hitler's mouth is a lie. When he says peace, he means war, and when he blasphemously uses the name of the Almighty, he means the power of evil, the fallen angel, Satan … whoever today still doubts the reality, the existence of demonic powers, has failed by a wide margin to understand the metaphysical background of this war. Behind the concrete, the visible events, behind all objective, logical considerations, we find the irrational element: The struggle against the demon, against the servants of the Antichrist.'

Hitler – Black Magician Or Medium?

All this talk of the devil and of Hitler being a medium for malevolent forces is naturally dismissed as fanciful by those conventional historians who see Nazi Germany as a socio-political phenomenon and Hitler as no more than a rabble-rousing demagogue and military opportunist. They are right when they suggest that there is no evidence that Hitler and his inner circle practised ritual magic or summoned demons to do their bidding. However, Hitler did awaken dark forces latent in the German soul and the nation succumbed to a mass neurosis which subverted all reason. But no one who marched under the black and red banners or cheered the goose-stepping storm troopers understood the true nature of those forces, nor could they

The Nuremberg Rallies were quasi-religious rites used to awaken the collective will of the Germans.

have resisted the lure of the malevolent Pied Piper who was leading them lemming-like to self-destruction, not unless they possessed a will equal to his. For the spell that Hitler unconsciously cast over the adoring masses was a form of magic, though it did not require a circle drawn on the ground, nor did it need incantations, robes or other occult paraphernalia. The phenomenon that was Nazi Germany was indeed a 'triumph of the will', to echo the title of Leni Riefenstahl's notorious Nazi propaganda film – it was the exercising of Hitler's domineering will over all others, it was his neurosis made manifest.

All those who fell into the orbit of the *Führer* testified to his personal magnetism and his penetrating gaze, which drained them of their will to resist. And it was not only the masses who submitted. Even his generals confessed to keeping their visits to headquarters to a minimum, for fear that their protests at his incessant meddling in military matters would be silenced by his overbearing personality.

Hitler's architect Albert Speer witnessed his mentor's ability to subdue his subordinates by sheer force of will on several occasions.

'They were all under his spell, blindly obedient and with no will of their own … to be in his presence for any length of time made me tired, exhausted and void.'

Even in the final days of the war, when Hitler's physical state had visibly degenerated, General Staff Officer Ulrich de Maizière observed that he 'had lost none of his demonic charisma'.

Magic Power

Hitler was not impressive or attractive as a man, but he possessed the power to enthral an audience, which he ruthlessly exploited for his own ends.

*'The power which has always started the greatest religions and po-
litical avalanches in history rolling has from time immemorial been
the magic power of the spoken word ... What I say is like an order
given under hypnosis.'*

Adolf Hitler (*Mein Kampf*)

Others, impervious to his personal magnetism, attributed Hitler's
appeal to supernatural forces. According to Nazi *Gauleiter* Her-
mann Rauschning:

*'One cannot help thinking of him as a medium. For most of the time,
mediums are ordinary, insignificant people. Suddenly, they are
endowed with what seems to be supernatural powers, which sets
them apart from the rest of humanity ... Once the crisis is passed,
they fall back again into mediocrity. It was in this way, beyond any
doubt, that Hitler was possessed by forces outside of himself – almost demonical forces of which the individual man, Hitler, was only
a temporary vehicle.'*

Invocation of Mars

As for the theatrical aspects of ceremonial magic, they were present in Germany, but they were not recognized at the time as such.
With their massed banners, martial music, arcane symbols and sol-
emn consecrating of flags the annual Nuremberg Rallies served as
a quasi-religious rite to awaken the collective will and invoke the
archetypes of the German psyche.

At dusk 200 searchlights beamed skywards to create what Albert
Speer called 'a cathedral of light', although nothing sacred was be-
ing enacted within this magic circle. Massed ranks of black-shirted
SS troops, brown-shirted SA stormtroopers, the Hitler Youth and

other groups listened enthralled to the sermon given by their mad messiah, who appealed to their basest instincts as well as their pride. But it was not the pride of achievement, it was the pride of Lucifer – arrogance, disdain, a false sense of superiority and an insatiable hunger for power.

Unleashing Evil

The Nazis required no assistance from the forces of darkness, because the evil they unleashed was entirely of their own making. The demons Hitler invoked were those festering in his own twisted psyche. He was not a magician in the traditional sense, but he instinctively exploited his oratorical gifts to manipulate the masses for his own selfish ends, appealing to their pride and their prejudices.

The nightmare that was Nazi Germany was the mob mentality writ large and it was all the more frightening because a nation that had given birth to some of the great intellects and artists of the modern age had been corrupted. Unaware of the nature of the forces that had been unleashed, the nation was unable to contain or control them and so was ultimately consumed by them. The Nazis were living proof, if needed, that evil is entirely man-made and that those who invoke the demonic or primal aspect of their nature are doomed to self-destruction. Unfortunately, the demons of our nature can cause untold suffering before they are finally subdued.

Goethe offered an insight into the nature of evil, which was to prove profoundly prophetic.

'The most fearful manifestation of the daemonic is when it is predominating in some individual character ... Such persons are not always the most eminent men, either in intellect or special gifts ... in vain does the more enlightened portion of mankind attempt to

throw suspicion upon them as dupes or as deceivers – the masses are attracted by them ... nothing can vanquish them but the Universe itself, with which they have begun the fray.'

THE CHURCH OF SATAN

'The devil is at his most dangerous when he is being charming.'

Professor Kumar

(character in *Night of the Demon*)

Anton LaVey sat at the organ in his basement chamber of horrors – the self-mockingly named Den of Iniquity – like Vincent Price in *The Abominable Dr Phibes*. He was surrounded by Satanic paraphernalia and life-sized marionettes dressed in fishnet stockings and fetish attire. As the candlelight threw mad shadows on the blood-red walls he

Anton LaVey emerges from a secret chamber behind a false fireplace in his study in San Francisco, 1967.

played old-time dance band tunes for the friends and hangers-on who had gathered to pay homage to the man they called 'The Black Pope'.

The year was 1986 and the founder of the Church of Satan was holding court in a large Victorian house near San Francisco's Golden Gate Park, which doubled as the organization's Satanic chapel. He was keen to prove that the devil can be a very beguiling fellow and a damn fine host. His basement-sanctuary-cum-nightclub boasted a collection of grimly fascinating artefacts, among them a genuine Aztec sacrificial knife, a torture hook used by the Spanish Inquisitors and a shrunken head from South America, donor unknown. All were relics from dead religions, their proud owner observed in a whisper as dry as parchment.

The outside of the building was painted Bible black with purple piping, so that it stood out like a bad tooth amidst the pastel-coloured town houses that lined the leafy suburban street. Its owner, too, was of equally unconventional appearance with his shaven head, goatee beard and penetrating gaze, not to mention his habitual funereal apparel. He was the very image of a modern Mephistopheles. Back in 1968 his strikingly sinister appearance had secured him the role he was born to play, that of the devil in Roman Polanski's horror movie *Rosemary's Baby*. But was the Church of Satan just a sideshow, a cynical con perpetrated by the former carnival showman, or was LaVey a true believer?

Off to a Good Start

Anton Szandor LaVey (1930–97) – born Howard Stanton Levey – devoted his life to spreading the black gospel of the Church of Satan, his own personal cult, which comprised thousands of members around the world at its height, including, it is said, celebrity converts Sammy Davis Jnr, Marc Almond and Marilyn Manson. Like it or not, it is now an officially-recognized religion in America, with charitable status. Even the US Army's chaplains are versed in its tenets, so they can minister to its members when they are under fire. Its founder admitted that he conceived the movement as a parody on orthodox religion, but the more he brooded on the need for a life-affirming alternative to the pacifist Christian credo, the more rapidly his natural cynicism crumbled, until he became a convert.

On 30 April 1966, Walpurgis Night, LaVey shaved his head in a manner that befitted the medieval executioners and declared the Church of Satan, or the 'temple of glorious indulgence', open for business. He exhibited a flair for self-promotion that would have done P.T. Barnum proud. In the years that followed, the devil rewarded him well. H acquired several luxury properties, a fleet of classic cars and even a yacht, so he could make a faster exit than Noah should an angry Jehovah take offence at his 'blasphemous' philosophy and plague the world with another Flood or, in the case of San Francisco, an earthquake.

Satan's Crazy Converts

But courting the devil also brought unwelcome attention in the shape of Jayne Mansfield's tragic death. On 29 July 1967 the Hollywood starlet was travelling in a car driven by her lover and lawyer Sam Brody when it was hit by a speeding truck. Mansfield suffered fatal head injuries and Brody was also killed. The only survivor was Mansfield's young daughter Mariska Hargitay (now the star of TV crime series Law and Order). Jayne Mansfield had gone against Brody's wishes by becoming an active member of the Church of Satan, which had provoked Brody to threaten to expose LaVey as a charlatan in the national press. LaVey responded by publicly cursing the lawyer and declaring that he would be dead within a year. He had warned Mansfield not to travel with Brody, but she had not taken the threat seriously. Not surprisingly the subsequent publicity attracted the 'wrong' sort of people to the cult.

LaVey was acutely aware that his immoral ideology would attract 'the crazies', as he called them. That is, neo-Nazis, Charles Manson's discarded disciples and the countless eccentrics who saw a conspiracy on every corner or heard voices urging them to kill in the devil's name. However, the majority of converts he claimed were attracted to Satanism because they needed to belong to something that gave meaning to their lives. They were the psychologically-damaged products of broken homes, drug addicts crawling from the wreckage of their dead-end lives or the disorientated children of devoutly religious parents who turned to LaVey, their dark guru, in adult life in order to exorcize their supposed sins.

Borrowed Belief

In the Black House, he shared his disciples' scorn for the people who lived routine, monotonous lives – the herd as he called them – but he equally despised those individuals who killed in the name of Satan to obtain notoriety.

'These people are not Satanists,' he once told a reporter. 'They are deranged. But no matter how many they do, they'll never catch up with the Christians. We have centuries of psychopathic killing in the name of God.'

When he hit the chat show circuit, he took the jibes against his outlandish 'lifestyle' in his stride. Amused by being compared to the Addams Family, he decorated his front parlour with fake cobwebs, joke shop skulls and a pet lion. The lion hadn't eaten a guest for months, he assured his visitors.

But for all his showmanship LaVey was in deadly earnest about his beliefs, even if they were second-hand goods that had been acquired from greater minds than his own – intellects such as the Russian-American novelist Ayn Rand, who formulated the philosophy of ethical egoism and objectivism, H.L. Mencken the acerbic American critic who opposed fundamentalist Christianity, the poet and visionary William Blake and of course, Friedrich Nietzsche, who originated the frequently misunderstood concept of the Superior Man.

Criticism of Crowley

Aleister Crowley, however, was not on LaVey's reading list. He accused 'the Beast' of having 'sold out' by denying that he was a Satanist and he criticized him for writing at interminable length on the subject of ritual magic. LaVey declared that he could have condensed it all into a single slim volume. Pretentiousness was one of the nine unforgivable sins in LaVey's self-penned *Satanic Bible*, a perennial best-seller that was published in 1969. The others were abstinence, spiritual daydreaming, self-deceit, unconditional love for those who do not deserve it, pacifism, the refusal to accept responsibility for one's actions, the assumption that man is more than an animal and is superior to all other creatures and blind religious observance.

Writing in his privately-printed newsletter *The Cloven Hoof*, LaVey attacked those in his own ranks who put their faith in the 'great teachings' of Aleister Crowley and the grand old masters of the Golden Dawn. There was clearly no love lost between the two old devils, with LaVey taking particular exception to Crowley's adoption of the number of the beast – 666 – which, he reminded his disciples, was of Christian origin. Both the Church and Crowley had given the devil a bad name and he would restore the old dog's reputation.

In *The Satanic Bible* and its companions, *The Satanic Witch* (1971) and *The Satanic Rituals* (1972), LaVey set out the principles on which his materialistic faith was founded.

The Devil's Doctrine

'The theory seems to be that as long as a man is a failure he is one of God's children, but that as soon as he succeeds he is taken over by the Devil.'

Henry Louis Mencken

According to LaVey, Satan is not a malevolent entity but an 'external projection of each individual's highest potential'. He is the personification of our carnal nature, a primitive archetypal aspect of ourselves which must not be suppressed or denied. True Satanists are therefore not evil, but individuals who dedicate themselves to the pursuit of pleasure and a life free of the restrictions and limitations that are imposed upon them by civilized society and its accomplice, orthodox religion. As such all Satanists are responsible for their own actions and cannot rely on a supernatural saviour to redeem them if they are untrue to themselves and the code by which they live. LaVey argued that orthodox religion was created by man, not God, so no one is obligated to live by its rules, especially since the laws and customs of its founders are no longer relevant in the modern world. The prophets and the priests created God in their own flawed image, envisaging Him as a cruel and capricious patriarch who can never be placated, because none of his children can live up to the standards of perfection that the Church imposes upon them. But, as LaVey has pointed out, no one has given the Church the authority to become the mediator between man and God or to impose its dogmas on society. It is, therefore, everyone's right to question this self-elected institution.

Unquestioning obedience and blind faith are contrary to the tenets of Satanism, which demands that individuals think for themselves and act according to their own conscience. LaVey contends that orthodox religion does not have a monopoly on the truth and he suggests that its ministers are just as capable of being cruel, self-serving and corrupt as the devil they claim to be at war with. Finally, he argues that it is unrealistic and unnatural to live in the material world and resist the pleasures it has to offer, in return for a mere promise of paradise.

The Satanic Bible

'Satanism is the only religion known to man that accepts man as he is.'

The Satanic Bible

In his preface to *The Satanic Bible* LaVey dismisses all occult literature as 'esoteric gibberish' and the 'brittle relics of frightened minds'. His credo, he states, does not aim to offend but is a belated expression of 'diabolical indignation' at the hypocrisy of organized religion. In contrast, Satanism encourages the gratification of the senses in the place of guilt, for the denial of pleasure is the root of all of our suffering and frustration.

LaVey did not claim to have channelled these commandments from a supernatural source. Instead, he acknowledged that he formulated his philosophy of assertive individualism from the writings of the fashionable intellectual elite with whom he wished to identify. But while he did not deny that the greater part of the book's text is a synthesis of other writers' ideas, and no less valid for being so, he begins to look as slippery as any snake-oil salesman as soon as one takes a closer look at the section he calls 'The Book of Satan'. The striking similarity between LaVey's pseudo-biblical polemic and the notorious 19th-century treatise on Social Darwinism,

Kelly Kalusha holds aloft his Satanic Bible as Hell, Michigan celebrates June 6, 2006, or 6/6/6.

Might Is Right – published under the pseudonym Ragnar Redbeard – makes a compelling case for accusing LaVey of plagiarism and cynicism. If he was too lazy even to paraphrase the core tenets of *Might Is Right* when he included them in his own 'black bible', one wonders what else was appropriated from other works without an acknowledgement.

A True Satanist

For those who might be intimidated by the abstract ideas in *The Satanic Bible*, LaVey added some homely wisdom from his carnival days, as well as his own observations on human nature drawn from personal experience. As a 16-year-old organist who had been hired to play at the Sunday morning Evangelist meetings, LaVey had witnessed hypocrisy at first hand. The men who now sat dutifully with their families praying and singing hymns had been lusting after half-naked girls the night before. His cynicism was compounded while working for the San Francisco police department as a crime scene photographer during the 1950s. After witnessing the brutality that human beings were capable of, and listening to the lies they told to save their own skins, he could not deny the existence of the devil within.

Had Anton LaVey been mad enough to imagine that he had the protection of Satan himself, he would surely have been tempted to offer the ultimate sacrifice, as Charles Manson and his followers had done. But he was a level-headed, calculating egotist, who was not going to risk everything he had gained by breaking the law, even to appease his infernal master. In fact, he exploited the law in order to ensure that his 'church' qualified for charity status. That made him a true Satanist in the eyes of his critics, for the very definition of a Satanist is a shameless self-serving schemer..

Selling Satan to the Masses

LaVey held Black Masses in his red and black painted apartment for the entertainment of the media, but no human blood was ever spilled in the devil's name. It was pure theatre for the curious, who were treated to the sight of a naked girl tied down on an altar while the congregation intoned their mantra, '*In nomine dei Satanas. Lucifer excelsi...*'

A hooded high priest then sprinkled a mixture of urine and semen from a censer shaped like a phallus. More invocations were accompanied by individual demands for whatever the members desired – a better-paid job, the attentions of a pretty girl or even the death of an enemy. LaVey confessed to journalists that his own black magic rituals were limited to requests for parking places and success in business, with the odd mischievous prank on the side. Christians and moralists were outraged by LaVey's shameless self-promotion and the inflammatory nature of his beliefs, but the truth of the matter is that they needed a devil to damn.

They needed to believe LaVey was the real deal or their own existence would lose its meaning. LaVey might have been Satan's best salesman but he made a valid point when he wrote, 'Satan has been the best friend the Church has ever had, as he kept it in business all these years!'

Chapter 5

Magic and Imagination

'Regarding the dreaded Necronomicon *of the mad Arab Abdul Alhazred – I must confess that both the evil volume and the accursed author are fictitious creatures of my own.'*

H.P. LOVECRAFT
(LETTER TO W.F. ANGER, 1934)

H.P. LOVECRAFT – THE CULT OF CTHULHU

In a dark and forbidding corner of one of London's more obscure occult bookshops stands a rack of extraordinary prints depicting hideous bug-eyed creatures that would give even the keenest naturalist nightmares. Should a customer take an interest in the display the balding, bespectacled owner will emerge from behind the counter to explain the significance of these loathsome beings. Such creatures, he will tell them, are not figments of the artist's fevered imagination but elemental spirits he encountered on the astral plane (see Austin Osman Spare, pages 171–3).

The fact that these eldritch horrors bear a striking resemblance to the winged and multi-tentacled entities described by the American pulp horror writer H.P. Lovecraft (1890–1937) is due, we are to understand, to the fact that Lovecraft had encountered these very same creatures during his uncommonly vivid dreams. Lovecraft dismissed them as mere 'Night-Gaunts', but then he felt compelled to do so, because he had a genuine fear of being overpowered and driven insane by the power of his own imagination. He did not want to die in a lunatic asylum as his father had done. Consequently, in letters to friends and admirers, the Providence-born writer readily admitted that his 'black pantheon' of nameless horrors was 'one hundred per cent fiction'.

And yet many practitioners of the forbidden arts argue that artists and writers possess an acute psychic sensitivity as a consequence of exploring the furthest regions of their imagination, which stimulates the areas of the brain associated with extrasensory perception – a latent faculty the mass of humanity might have lost during the course of our evolution.

Cosmic Library

Psychics often speak of the Akashic Records – a virtual library containing the entire knowledge of the world that one can browse in sleep or during meditation. Every thought and every event in our history is said to be documented there, accessible to all who seek it. A voracious reader and dreamer such as Lovecraft would have visited this source of all knowledge in his dreams but may not have had any memory of having done so.

He certainly knew the power of visualization and the mind's capacity to manifest archetypal creatures from the depths of the subconscious.

As a child of seven or eight he admitted to being so intoxicated with the mythology of the ancient Greeks that he 'half believed' in the existence of their gods and nature spirits.

'Once I firmly thought I beheld some kind of sylvan creatures dancing under autumnal oaks, a kind of "religious experience" as true in its way as the subjective ecstasies of a Christian ... I have seen hoofed Pan ...'

Modern-day occultists believe that Lovecraft was a visionary who unconsciously accessed the lower astral worlds, which are inhabited by a multitude of archetypal manifestations of our unconscious fears, and that these provided the inspiration for his Cthulhu Mythos – a fictional universe that Lovecraft originally created for his own stories. The Cthulhu Mythos has since been used by a number of other authors of horror stories. Places, names and inhabitants crop up again and again in different books, thereby adding substance to this shared dimension. Mythos stories often refer to the 'Great Old Ones', a race of malevolent gods who were cast out of our world

H.P. Lovecraft on a mock-up of the cover of Weird Tales: his influence on occultism has been immense.

for practising black magic. They now dwell in a sixth dimension in the spaces between worlds, and are 'ever ready to take possession of this earth again'.

Childhood Nightmares

In a letter to friend Virgil Finlay dated October 1936, Lovecraft recalled his childhood nightmares in which black, faceless, lean, 'rubbery things' with wings and tails would carry him over 'dead and horrible' cities.

Seventy years after his death H.P. Lovecraft continues to exert an all-pervasive influence on fantasy fiction and popular culture, because the world he created was so richly conceived and vividly described that it holds a morbid fascination for writers, artists, film-makers and connoisseurs of the macabre the world over.

His Cthulhu Mythos, with its dark pantheon of ancient gods and loathsome eldritch horrors, has inspired several generations of authors and artists including H.R. Giger (creator of the creature in *Alien*) and illustrator Alan Moore, as well as generating a slew of comic books, computer games and countless Heavy Metal anthems. Sadly, though, there have been few films worthy of his fervid imagination.

The key to Lovecraft's enduring appeal is his creation of a very credible alternative reality, in which monstrous evil lurks on the threshold of our world, waiting to prey upon those foolish enough to invoke it. His fictional town of Arkham and its environs, in which many of the stories are set, was based on real locations near his home in Providence, New England, which lent the turn of the century tales an air of genteel melancholy and decay.

So convincing was he in chronicling the lore and mythology of this claustrophobic nightmarish world – despite a professed lack of interest in all things supernatural – that the dark gods of his imagination have now taken on a life of their own and are being worshipped by several demonic cults who believe in their actual existence.

The *Necronomicon*

Incredible though it may seem, several cults have adopted Lovecraft's fictional grimoire, the *Necronomicon*, as their black bible, despite his admission that the 'hellish & forbidden volume is an imaginative conception of mine ...' and its 'author', Abdul Alhazred the mad Arab, has been thought of as a real person (letter to Robert Bloch, author of *Psycho*, 9 May 1933). It is thought that the name (which has no origin in Arabic) was Lovecraft's pet name for his youthful self, whom he saw as a voracious reader (All-Has-Read). Quite apart from Lovecraft's own admission that the name came to him in a dream, there is the undeniable fact that no mention was made of this 8th-century text before Lovecraft alluded to it more than 1,000 years later. Moreover, in his early stories Lovecraft contradicts himself as to its contents and the nature of the work – is it a witches' Book of Shadows or a witchfinder's handbook? Its frustrating vagueness and constant deferral to other elusive texts is characteristic of fictional grimoires and would immediately arouse the suspicions of serious occultists.

Nevertheless, one group of devotees, the Esoteric Order of Dagon – who claim to have established lodges in Australia, the United States and Europe – have stated that while they do not necessarily believe in the existence of the 'Great Old Ones', they find the iconography of Lovecraft's world to be a useful stimulus for gaining access to areas of their own subconscious. It is believed that dreams may offer a glimpse of a greater reality, even though they might not possess physical substance.

This reality can also be accessed in the waking state, through a form of guided visualization that members of the Western esoteric tradition call Pathworking and Jungian psychologists refer to as 'active imagination'. The term Pathworking comes from the Kabbalists, who developed the technique as a means of exploring the symbolic landscape of the psyche, as represented by the interconnecting paths and spheres on the Tree of Life, the central glyph of the Kabbalistic system.

In this way individuals who are attracted to Lovecraft's timeless world could use his primal gods in a ritual visualization that would awaken the atavistic forces that exist in a dreamless sleep between dimensions.

Influence

The influence of H.P. Lovecraft on modern practical occultism cannot be overestimated. One of his most ardent admirers was Anton LaVey, founder and high priest of the Church of Satan, who chose to consecrate each meeting of his sect with an incantation from Lovecraft's *The Horror At Red Hook*.

Kenneth Grant, a disciple of Aleister Crowley, believed that Lovecraft was a natural adept who was drawn to the nightmarish Qlippothic shadow realms of the Tree in his dreams, but being unfamiliar with the Kabbalistic system he was not able to contextualize what he had experienced, so he constructed his own fictional nether world that was inhabited by the creatures he had seen.

The very elusiveness of the *Necronomicon* is, of course, part of its appeal. Its origins have been obscured by the many veiled references to it in the works of other fantasy writers with whom Lovecraft corresponded, among them Robert Bloch, Clark Ashton Smith and Robert E. Howard (creator of Conan). But although

Lovecraft had been invited to pen the accursed work himself to satisfy fans, he admitted that it was beyond him and that no book could live up to the legend.

'I wish I had the time and imagination to assist in such a project ... one can never produce anything even a tenth as terrible and impressive as one can awesomely hint about.'

H.P. Lovecraft (*Collected Letters*)

Lovecraft proclaimed himself a 'mechanistic materialist' and he professed disbelief in the supernatural, yet he was both awed and terrified by the idea that as a writer he might have developed an acute psychic sensitivity and so be able to access the surreal symbolic landscape of the unconscious. He shrank from a world in which his fears could take form, fears which literally haunted him throughout his brief, unhappy life.

Philosophy

In his most celebrated short story, 'The Call of Cthulhu', Lovecraft expounded his own nihilistic philosophy. It was wrought from an inherent neurosis and frustrated literary ambitions and exacerbated, presumably, by an increasing fear that the creatures of his imagination were now beginning to take possession of him.

'The most merciful thing in the world, I think, is the inability of the human mind to correlate all its contents ... some day the piecing together of dissociated knowledge will open up such terrifying vistas of reality, and of our frightful position therein that we shall either go mad from the revelation or flee from the deadly light into the peace and safety of a new dark age.'

While the *Necronomicon* is without a shadow of a doubt a fictional creation, a number of fake editions have been published in recent years by fans and less scrupulous occultists in order to satisfy the demand, and indeed need, for such a Stygian tome. Some of these small press publications are clearly cobbled together from the fictional excerpts Lovecraft included in his stories and are as harmless as a Gandalf grimoire, but other less scrupulous individuals have included genuine magical rituals without any warning of the inherent dangers that await the unwary.

Genuine magicians will say that even if the dark gods and demons of Lovecraft's stories had originally been insubstantial projections of his imagination, any form of prolonged meditation on such things would effectively empower them with life. If that is true, the collective obsession of successive generations of horror addicts might have given these eldritch horrors real substance by now.

THE MAGICAL ARTS – AUSTIN OSMAN SPARE

'Life is haunted – I see faces of the so-called dead everywhere...'
Austin Osman Spare

The history of art has included some bizarre examples of 'self expression', from Picasso's distorted abstracts and Dali's dreamscapes to Damien Hirst's pickled cow and Tracey Emin's unmade bed. None, however, can compare with the disturbing imagery drawn by occult artist Austin Osman Spare (1886–1956), who threw aside a promising career to paint the surreal creatures of the astral dimension, a realm he explored using his own psychic powers.

Spare was born within sight and sound of the teeming streets of

In his teens, Austin Spare was declared an artist of genius by the great and the good of London's art world.

Whitechapel, soon to be haunted by Jack the Ripper. His father was a low-ranking policeman on the periphery of the hunt for England's first serial killer and his mother was by all accounts a rather forbidding figure who denied her son the love he craved.

But Spare's father was supportive of his artistic ambitions. He recognized that his son was a precocious talent and he proudly submitted samples of his work to the Royal Academy, which were exhibited while Spare was still in his teens. Acclaim was swift and unanimous, with artists such as John Singer Sargent declaring the boy a genius.

But it was not acceptance as an artist that Spare sought so desperately. Neglected by his mother, he fell under the influence of an elderly neighbour and fortune-teller – his 'witch-mother', as he called her. She showed him how he could use dream imagery as a source of inspiration for his art and also how to access the symbolic landscape of his subconscious mind through visualization. He continued to produce conventional portraits, which attracted rave reviews, but it was the astral world and its elemental inhabitants that fascinated him throughout his life. He claimed to have communicated with a spirit guide, attended witches' sabbats and explored fantastic, futuristic cities in his 'dream body', using astral projection. But he admitted that even his artistic skills were inadequate to convey the other-worldly nature of the architecture, which invites comparison with that described by author H.P. Lovecraft.

Losing Touch with Reality

Spare's occult studies and his art became inseparable, but the deeper he delved into the darker regions of the subconscious, the more unsettling his visions became. His sketches present a gallery of grotesques that no worldly artist could have created – headless torsos writhing in exquisite agony and elemental 'insects' crawling from between the cracks in consciousness. Some called him mad and shunned him, despite his prodigious talent, but others indulged him, hoping that somehow they might be able to share his visionary gifts by clinging to his coat-tails, listening to his rambling monologues or taking the same drugs. But such experiences are subjective and cannot be shared. It requires a certain mindset and disposition to tear the veil between this world and the next and there are few who can slip effortlessly into this other state of being and return to waking consciousness as sane as they left it.

H.P. Lovecraft was able to distinguish between his nightmares and reality, using his experiences as the foundation of his fantasy, but the tragedy of Austin Osman Spare was that he was not willing to return to reality. He was consumed by the idea that he could stay in the astral dimension and at the same time capture its frightening enormity on canvas.

'By turning my head involuntarily, I can always see my alter ego, familiars or the gang of elementals that partly constitute my being,' he told *Leader* magazine in 1948.

The trouble was nobody else could see these creatures and those who were not repulsed by their appearance in his paintings thought that he must be insane to even conceive of such abominations.

Association with Crowley

In 1905 Spare published his first book, *Earth Inferno*, in which he compared the material world to hell itself and urged his fellow artists to turn their backs on materialism and seek a greater reality through the medium of automatic drawing (see box, pages 176–7). This was a technique whereby they could channel the creative muse independently of the brain and so draw free from the restrictions of style or learned technique – a suggestion that naturally offended the establishment. He also became notorious in Bohemian society for performing 'magic tricks', such as exorcizing a ghost from a cleric's haunted home and conjuring rain from a cloudless sky, but his wild-eyed appearance and increasing use of drugs left the drawing-room set decidedly uncomfortable in his presence.

George Bernard Shaw summed him up by saying, 'Spare's medicine is too strong for the average man.'

It was only a matter of time before Spare's art and activities attracted the interest of Aleister Crowley, who was impressed by the young artist's ability to capture the essence of creatures he too had encountered on the astral plane. In 1910 Crowley commissioned several sketches from Spare for his magazine *The Equinox* and he invited the young artist to join his magic circle Argenteum Astrum (Order of the Silver Star). But the two men had very different temperaments. Crowley was an overbearing egotist who demanded obedience and adoration, while Spare was a solitary figure who was content to work quietly and inwardly on his own. Spare was repulsed by the idea that Crowley was grooming him as a sexual slave and Crowley grew impatient with the young man's pranks, which included baking cakes from horse manure and delaying his commitment to the circle on the grounds that he could not afford the ceremonial robe. But what prised them apart in the end was Spare's refusal to acknowledge Crowley as his intellectual and magical superior. Spare's parting insult was to compare 'The Great Beast' to an unemployed Italian pimp. They never spoke again.

Sigils

In 1913 Spare published his first volume of occult philosophy, *The Book of Pleasure (Self-love)*, subtitled *The Psychology of Ecstasy*, in which he described how one could evoke beings from the subconscious using the animal life force released during sex. He also explained how to cast spells using sigils, which contracted incantations and affirmations into a single symbol by eliminating superfluous letters. The remaining letters would then be drawn on parchment or worn as a talisman. The idea behind sigils was that one can impress one's desires upon the subconscious with symbols but not with language. If the object of the magical operation can be condensed into a single symbol then it is possible to programme the subconscious to bring the desired action into being as a blueprint, or prototype, at the astral level. It then assumes substance in the physical world, where it will manifest by power of the will.

This method might have worked in theory, but when Spare attempted to demonstrate it in public the result was less than impressive. According to the author Francis X. King, Spare declared his intention to manifest rose petals from the ether and to that end he began to chant a mantra while waving the requisite sigil in the air, his features contorted with the effort of will. Moments later the ceiling caved in and gallons of untreated sewage from a burst pipe drenched the participants in effluent.

During the First World War Spare served as an official war artist. When he found himself posted to Egypt, he became enamoured of the Egyptian deities and was introduced to the meditation technique their high priests called Assuming The God Form. In 1921 he published a second volume of magical techniques under the title *The Focus of Life*, in which he described his own version of this ancient technique, which he renamed the Death Posture. It was later developed into the practice of chaos magic.

The Final Years

Then in 1927 Spare poured forth a seething diatribe against the sycophants and hypocrites of the art world, and society in general, in *Anathema of Zos: The Sermon to the Hypocrites*, which he claimed had been channelled using automatic writing and was therefore beyond criticism. The sins of the modern world, he said, were compromise and blind acceptance of the mundane. Man was capable of much more, but only a visionary such as himself could see what the rest of society was missing because of its blinkered view of reality.

He then grew more reclusive, eccentric, intolerant and alienated from the artistic establishment, whom he saw as insincere and cliquish.

'I turned my back on fame and continued unmolested my quests into the unknown realms, my natural stoicism supporting me in times of want,' he wrote.

With few commissions to supplement his income he was reduced to living in a grimy basement in South London, surrounded by the stray cats he adopted from the street. Then during the Second World War the basement took a direct hit from a German bomb, which left Spare paralysed down the right-hand side of his body. Miraculously, through strength of will he regained the use of his right arm and taught himself to draw again, but it took three years and all of his strength. He also began work on what was to be his *magnum opus*, a modern grimoire, the *Zos Kia Cultus*.

But he was now reduced to living on a few shillings a week. He repaired radios for beer money and painted portraits of movie stars from the pages of magazines to save himself from starving. Dressed in a heavy overcoat and boots, with a shock of white hair and the rank odour of stale cigarettes and beer completing the effect, he became a virtual tramp, a local curiosity to be goaded and teased by children and pitied by his neighbours. But his occult powers were apparently undiminished. When two curiosity seekers braved the filthy basement in which he was living and challenged him to demonstrate his abilities he is said to have conjured up a black cloud of such malevolent intensity that both onlookers fled for fear of their lives.

Spare died in 1956, forgotten by the art world but regarded by occultists as a significant figure and the father of chaos magic.

AUTOMATIC DRAWING

The following extract is taken from an article written by Spare and published in *Form* magazine in 1916.

'Automatic drawing, one of the simplest of psychic phenomena, is a means of characteristic expression, and if used with courage and honesty, of recording subconscious activities in the mind ...

'The dangers of this form of expression come from prejudice and personal bias of such nature as fixed intellectual conviction or personal religion (intolerance) ... Automatic drawings can be obtained by such methods as concentrating on a Sigil or by any means of exhausting mind and body pleasantly in order to obtain a condition of non-consciousness.

'The Hand must be trained to work freely and without control, by practice in making simple forms with a continuous involved line without afterthought, i.e. its intention should just escape consciousness.

'Drawings should be made by allowing the hand to run freely with the least possible deliberation. In time shapes will be found to evolve, suggesting conceptions, forms and ultimately having personal or individual style.

'The mind in a state of oblivion, without desire towards re-flection or pursuit of materialistic intellectual suggestions, is in a condition to produce successful drawings of one's personal ide-as, symbolic in meaning and wisdom. By this means sensation may be visualized.'

RIPPING YARNS –
DENNIS WHEATLEY

A nubile young girl writhes naked on a black satin cloth embroidered with an inverted pentagram, her wrists and ankles tied at each corner of the altar on which her virgin blood is to be shed. Behind the altar, framed by two black candles and brandishing a ceremonial sacrificial dagger, the high priest of a Satanic cult invokes his infernal master.

Such iconic imagery could have been taken from any one of a number of Hammer horror films made in the 1960s and early 1970s, when society's interest in black magic and occultism was at its height. It was a time when the hippie dream of the psychedelic Sixties had been shattered by the shock of the Charles Manson cult murders and the permissive society was threatening the moral order imposed by organized religion, whose authority was in rapid decline. Sex, drugs and rock music were all perceived as symptoms of the devil's increasing influence, but the unlikely agent provocateur at the centre of this diabolical interest in the dark side of the occult was not a black magician but a middle-aged former British counter-intelligence officer turned author, Dennis Wheatley.

Wheatley had no first-hand knowledge or experience of the occult, but he decided that the subject would make a ripping yarn. And he was right. His melodramatic prose style, corny *Boy's Own* action scenes and politically incorrect prejudices proved no barrier to commercial success.

Readers lapped up the pacey pulp thrillers with their heady doses of sadism, sex and pseudo scholarship, set amidst a cosy world of country house soirées and smoke-filled gentlemen's clubs.

Wheatley's heroes are all cross-carrying Christians whose faith, friendship and fearlessness always wins the day against the shifty Satanists, who are invariably somewhat repugnant foreigners.

Private Beliefs

Privately the author considered Christianity a joyless religion and preferred the life-enhancing philosophies of the East. The one occasion on which he called on the devil to help him win at cards was apparently sufficient to warn him off for life. He claims that he began winning hand after hand against the odds and had to make a conscious effort to lose in order to break the spell. Unfortunately, we will never know how much the episode owes to Wheatley's rich imagination.

The first of his lurid black magic novels, *The Devil Rides Out*, became a rapid best-seller in 1934 and by the time of his death in 1977 'Britain's occult uncle', as his biographer has named him, had sold in excess of 50 million copies. It is Wheatley's descriptions of devil-inspired debauchery in such novels as *The Devil Rides Out* and *They Used Dark Forces* that are largely responsible for igniting the public consciousness and stimulating the wild imaginings of the more sensationalistic tabloid press. But there is little evidence that Satanic cults and covens ever existed, at least not in the highly theatrical form in which they are portrayed by Wheatley.

Over-the-counter Magic

In her rigorous investigation of the Satanic sex abuse scare of the 1990s, Professor Jean La Fontaine made the observation that many of the alleged victims had generated false memories drawn from popular occult fiction, specifically the novels of Dennis Wheatley, who had promulgated the idea of a global Satanic conspiracy.

Nevertheless, the novels were a handy source of forbidden lore for a generation who had neither the means nor the inclination to make a pilgrimage to the East in search of wisdom. It was easier to take LSD and dress their orgies up in the trappings of devil worship.

Although Wheatley professed no serious interest in Satanism, he lent credibility to his salacious tales by consulting a number of experts on the subject, including Aleister Crowley, Rollo Ahmed and Montague Summers. Consequently his detailed descriptions of ceremonial magic, conjurations, curses and invocations offered any curious adolescent a working knowledge of the Black Arts for the price of a packet of cigarettes. They had only to browse through their local market stalls and antique shops to pick up the required paraphernalia, trinkets and charms and they would then be able to conduct their own diabolical rites.

A Warning to Others

But the secrets revealed in Wheatley's books were not harmless con-jurer's tricks from the local magic shop, nor the relics of a more superstitious age. If they were practised by the uninitiated, the imag-inative and the immature they had the potential to wreak psycholog-ical havoc, especially if drugs were also involved. Wheatley made his own views on the subject known during a rare radio interview.

'Nine-tenths of them are phonies. To call down the powers of evil is a life-time's job. Most of these people are in it just for sexual orgies and the dope traffic. We should investigate the powers of the human mind, certainly, but this monkeying about with unknown forces is dangerous for the weak-minded. I've known people neglect their wives and families and end up in the loony-bin.'

As he told the *Daily Express* in March 1975:

'I get on average a dozen letters a week from people who suspect that they're possessed by the Devil ... I don't myself believe in the traditional picture of a hooved and horned Devil with a tail. That is absurd. But I do believe very definitely in a power of light ... and in a power of darkness in which things decay and die and which is

a power of evil. I haven't the least doubt that it is possible to evoke this evil power of darkness. You can do it when you mean to do it – for instance by praying: "May Uncle Roger die soon, so that I can get at his money." Equally by dabbling in the occult when we don't know what the consequences can be, we may be stirring up evil forces.'

As a child at preparatory school on the Kent coast, just prior to the Great War, Wheatley saw his first ghost, 'a ghastly face', whose appearance he blamed on the housemaster, who had been conducting seances. After that Wheatley vowed never to become involved in a magical ceremony or a seance. But he would write about the subject, in order to warn everyone of the dangers of tampering with unknowable and uncontrollable forces.

THE EXORCIST

When director William Friedkin's film *The Exorcist* was first screened in 1974, audiences were more than terrified – they were traumatized. Some ran screaming from the cinema without stopping to demand their money back. Others vomited in the aisles. Those who managed to suppress their revulsion by telling themselves that it was only a movie were disturbed by nightmares for months, even years, afterwards. But this was not just another Hollywood horror movie. What made *The Exorcist* so nauseously effective was the claim that the story of a young girl's demonic possession was allegedly based on a true, well-documented case.

Author Peter Blatty based his best-selling novel of the same name on a report in *The Washington Post*, which detailed a case that had occurred in a suburb of the capital back in 1949. A 14-year-old boy identified by the fictitious name of Robbie Mannheim had exhibited the classic symptoms of demonic possession following the death of his beloved Aunt Harriet. Robbie was an only child who was doted upon and indulged by his aunt, a Christian spiritualist, who introduced her nephew to the Ouija board and encouraged his belief in ghosts. Then on Saturday 15 January 1949 their dangerous game took a nasty turn. They heard a loud dripping sound but couldn't find the source. A framed picture of Jesus was seen to shake and other sounds such as rapping noises and scratches were heard. Robbie's father, Karl, became so agitated that he ripped up the floorboards and pulled panels from the wall in an effort to catch the rats he believed were responsible for the noise. But no rodents were found.

Nearly two weeks later Aunt Harriet died and Robbie became sullen and isolated. In desperation he tried to contact her spirit by using the Ouija board and that is when he supposedly became possessed by a malevolent entity and the house became the centre of poltergeist activity. The family was treated to the sound of squeaky shoes in uninhabited rooms while furniture and household objects moved about of their own accord. Robbie became the focus of more inexplicable phenomena at school, when desk lids banged and moved without the aid of human hands. Then, to the horror of the boy's family and other witnesses, words imprinted themselves on his body and what sounded like demons could be heard speaking through him.

A Job for the Church

All attempts to find a rational explanation failed after psychiatrists and medical specialists ran exhaustive tests. They could find no cause for Robbie's symptoms. With the conventional cures exhausted, the family appealed to their priest, the Reverend Luther Miles Schulze.

A night alone with the boy was enough to convince Schulze that the only hope of a cure lay in conducting an exorcism. But the Anglican rite was evidently not effective enough, because the phenomena continued to plague Robbie and his family, so the case was referred to a Roman Catholic priest who conducted a second exorcism at the Jesuit institution in Georgetown University Hospital. But the ritual had to be postponed when Robbie assaulted the priest, leaving the poor man with a wound requiring extensive stitches.

After the boy returned home other phenomena occurred, including the appearance of the words 'St Louis' on his chest. St Louis was the city in which Aunt Harriet had died. The words appeared in blood, which suggests that Robbie might have scratched them into his own skin with his fingernails. But after witnessing the boy's bed rocking violently and more objects flying through the air, the Reverend Raymond Bishop of St Louis University, and the Reverend William S. Bowdern of College Church, concluded that only a no-holds-barred exorcism would cast the demons from their host. They sought permission from their archbishop, who approved the exorcism on condition that Bowdern recorded the details in a diary and kept the location secret. Bowdern agreed to the archbishop's terms and asked the Reverend Walter Halloran and William Van Roo to assist him in the rite, which was to be performed in the psychiatric wing of the Alexian Brothers Hospital.

'It's Over'

According to Halloran's diary, Robbie's spasms became so violent that he lashed out at the priest, breaking his nose. More words and more wounds appeared on the boy's body and his bed shook violently, after which objects began to fly across the room. Finally, Robbie verbally abused the two priests and then spat at them, but they kept their heads. If there were demons inside Robbie they were tenacious devils, because they refused to leave despite the priests' best efforts. Exhausted, they left the hospital that night determined to return to the fray when their energies were replenished. If the reports are to be believed, it took a further thirty or so sessions before the infernal entities fled their host. During the final exorcism Halloran uttered the magic words '*Christus Domini*', at which point a thunderous report echoed through every room in the building, leaving the boy with no memory of the events.

'It's over,' he told the priests, as if he had tired of a game he had been playing. And maybe he had been doing just that.

Not Demons

Long after *The Exorcist* had scared an entire generation of moviegoers out of its wits, author Mark Opsasnick made what is arguably the most thorough investigation of the case. He concluded that Robbie was an emotionally unstable attention seeker who had pretended to be possessed in order to avoid having to go to a school he hated. Opsasnick detailed many inconsistencies in the initial reports written by the family's clergyman, the Reverend Luther Miles Schulze. He also came to the conclusion that the priest had wildly exaggerated the supernatural elements of the investigation. Even the Reverend Halloran had suspected that the boy had merely mimicked the Latin phrases he had heard the priests repeating. However, it is believed that genuine poltergeist phenomena can be caused by neurotic or emotional adolescents, who involuntarily discharge kinetic energy which causes objects to move and interferes with the electrical supply. The associated events are frightening to watch but they are not caused by demons, nor are they particularly dangerous.

On the other hand, subjecting a disturbed person to the physical and psychological assault of exorcism is both irresponsible and highly dangerous.

According to several leading psychiatrists who examined the case, the death of the boy's aunt and his denial of her death is likely to have produced a number of psychological disorders ranging from Automatism (involuntary physical actions), Obsessive Compulsive Disorder (irrational fears, obsessions and compulsions) and even Gilles de la Tourette's Syndrome (which produces uncontrollable screaming and foul language).

In recent years the Catholic Church has refused to endorse the practice of exorcism, while the Church of England has condemned it as 'extremely dubious'. Legal experts have also spoken out against it, saying that it feeds 'neurosis to a neurotic' while Mark Opsasnick's considered opinion was that, 'Those involved saw what they were trained to see.'

IN TWO MINDS

'Demons do not exist any more than gods do, being only the products of the psychic activity of man.'

Sigmund Freud

Orthodox science naturally rejects any suggestion that there is a spirit realm and that the inhabitants of this dimension are able to influence us for better or worse be they ghosts, angels or demons. The world of science explains all kinds of psychic phenomena, including demonic possession and inner voices of a divine and demonic nature, by proposing that our brains contain two distinct aspects of our personality. As a result of experiments and observations conducted during the 1960s, the pioneers of split brain research, Americans Roger Sperry and Robert Ornstein, concluded that the left half of the brain deals with language and logical thought processes whereas the right side is the origin of intuition and perception. In psychologically sound individuals one of these halves, or hemispheres, is dominant and the other is passive. However, under exceptional circumstances – in times of extreme stress or deep relaxation, for instance, or when there is a physical severing of the cerebral hemispheres – these two 'selves' can operate independently. In one striking example, a patient tried to embrace his wife with his right arm while his left hand pushed her away (the right side of the brain controls the left side of the body and vice versa).

Such behaviour may account for many cases of alleged demonic possession and the 'dual nature of man' that is mythologized in the eternal struggle between good and evil. But it also raises the possibility that paranormal powers and magical abilities might be the result of a physical or psychological 'short circuit', to borrow a phrase coined by occult investigator Colin Wilson. As Wilson has pointed out in his highly influential books *The Occult* and *Mysteries*, many psychics obtained their powers after suffering an emotional trauma, an electric shock or a physical blow to the head. People who perceive the world entirely through the left side of their brains see magic and supernatural phenomena as illogical and unrealistic, but those individuals who have developed their intuitive powers, such as artists and musicians, often experience a cumulative effect, with episodes of precognition becoming more common.

And if such abilities can exist then is it not reasonable to assume that mental energy, when focused upon a certain aim and energized by the will, could bring about change, such as a transformation in matter or in the minds of others?

It is a process that we do not fully understand so therefore we call it magic. Wilson suggests that the pressures of civilization – the mundane and routine nature of modern life – might have contributed to the development of the left half of our brains at the expense of the right, thereby weakening our connection with nature and the supernatural or spirit world.

ALAN MOORE – A MODERN MERLIN

'An artist or writer is the closest thing in the contemporary world to a shaman.'

In November 1993, on his fortieth birthday, world-renowned comic artist and writer Alan Moore, creator of *The League of Extraordinary Gentlemen*, *Watchmen*, *From Hell* and *V For Vendetta* confessed to being a practising magician. He believed that making the transition from artist to magician was a logical progression but he nevertheless expected howls of derision from the popular press, pitying looks from his long-suffering family and groans from his legion of fans, who would think he had finally gone over the edge. Too many drugs and too much Hawkwind (English space rock group) they would say.

But those who were acquainted with Moore knew better. With his grizzled grey beard and long bedraggled hair he could pass for an aging hippie, but this was the man who almost single-handedly reinvented the medium of comics for a new adult audience, bringing literacy, politics and a masterly visual sensibility to a once crude and derided craft. Comics and their recent multi-million dollar movie adaptations are no longer for kids.

Alan Moore is a modern Merlin, the natural successor to Crowley, Spare and Blake.

In fact, the word 'comic' is now passé thanks almost entirely to Moore, who can take much of the credit for the rise of a new art form, the graphic novel, in which stereotypical superheroes have become subversives in a sinister, neo-fascist society that could never have existed in the same universe as that inhabited by the original square-jawed Legion of Superheroes of Marvel and DC.

Catching the Bug

Moore is a modern Merlin, the natural successor to Crowley, Spare and Blake. But this British-born artist has the advantage of having both feet on terra firma, having endured the hard knocks of the real world and having had to scramble for a living. Yet despite his wealth and fame he continues to live in a modest terraced house in Northampton, where magical artefacts and occult volumes tumble from overcrowded shelves or vie for space with records, videos, comic book collectibles and memorabilia. His house has been described as an occult bookshop under continual renovation.

As one bemused visitor observed, 'This is clearly a man who spends little time on the material plane.'

Moore's obsession with the occult was triggered by a casual remark he wrote in his first highly influential and groundbreaking graphic novel, *From Hell*, which retold the story of the Whitechapel murders perpetrated by Jack the Ripper.

'One word balloon in From Hell *completely hijacked my life ... A character says something like, "The one place gods inarguably exist is in the human mind". After I wrote that, I realized I'd accidentally made a true statement, and now I'd have to rearrange my entire life around it. The only thing that seemed to really be appropriate was to become a magician.'*

Early Explorations

Like Blake and Spare before him, Moore believes that magic is an art and that all art forms are a form of magic. Both involve the manipulation of symbols, words or images to achieve changes in consciousness. The act of writing, he says, is a spell of sorts. Thoughts, ideas and names are all conveyed by the medium of words and that is why words have power.

'I found that I couldn't progress any further with writing by strict rationality. If I wanted to go further with my writing, make it more intense, more powerful, make it say what I wanted it to say, I had to take a step beyond technique and rational ideas about writing, into something that was trans-rational if you will, this being magic.'

Over the following months Moore immersed himself in the works of Aleister Crowley, mastered the tarot and delved into the mysteries of the Qabalah (the alternative spelling indicating the Western magical form of the tradition). His first revelation was the realization that magic occurs on a mental plane to which we all have access when we heighten our awareness of a Greater Reality beyond our mundane or everyday minds. To navigate this virtual reality the magician needs a system that provides a map, the most practical being the Qabalistic glyph known as the Tree of Life. In his early explorations Moore had used drugs to attain an altered state but he quickly realized that this dulled the senses and led to disorientation.

But even without psychedelics he still found these initial forays a frightening experience.

'You call out the names in this strange incomprehensible language, and you're looking into the glass and there appears to be this little man talking to you. It just works.'

Reality of Imagination

Less than two months after his 'coming out' party, Moore had what he considered to be his first magical experience. He was performing a ritual with a friend when they were both struck by what felt like a non-lethal bolt of lightning.

'It felt like an extraordinary intelligence passed through both of us ... I was quite prepared to admit that this may have all been complete hallucination, except for the fact that I had somebody else with me who was experiencing the same things.'

Even though he readily admits that he didn't always understand what he saw or encountered, he knew he had to continue until he could make sense of his experiences. To assist him on the astral plane he adopted an ancient Roman divinity, the serpent god Glycon. He knew Glycon was a false god but he adopted this particular deity anyway, because a snake is a powerful image.

Moore did not need to be told that imagination is the key to occult experience and that the world of the imagination is not to be confused with fantasy, but is another reality. Magic, he explained, was a method for dealing with the invisible world, the world of ideas from which everything in the material world has its origin. The divinities and demons of our ancestors were the names they gave to inner forces they did not yet understand and so they personified them to help them interact with these inner attributes. The world of ideas is therefore more real than the material world, even though it is not a physical reality. Ideas, Moore reminds us, are immortal, immaterial and universal, but they remain elusive and impenetrable without a system to give them structure in our minds, and that is what ritual magic can offer.

To assist him on the astral plane, Moore adopted an ancient Roman deity, the serpent god Glycon.

'The most peculiar entities that I believe myself to have encountered, including presences which appeared to be genuine Gods, have seemed to me to be at once utterly alien or Other, and at the same time have seemed to be a part of myself.'

Inevitably, his insights and experiences inspired a new comic series – *Promethea*, the story of a teenage girl possessed by a pagan goddess.

'I wanted to be able to do an occult comic that didn't portray the occult as a dark, scary place, because that's not my experience of it.'

Exploring the Paths

Moore is clearly no dabbler but an adept and one who will inevitably attain a high degree of insight, because he has the humility that Crowley and his more psychologically unstable forerunners lacked. Speaking of his experiences exploring the paths and spheres of the Qabalistic Tree, he confessed:

'The sixth is as high as I've ventured as yet and people who know a lot more about it than I do have advised me that there is less and less to actually experience the higher you get, while the dangers get more and more severe. Kether, the highest allegedly attainable point, is in one sense nothing more than the initial concept of existence itself ... There may be magicians who have gone there, but if so, they never came back.'

God, as envisaged by the founders of the Western religions, has no place in this pantheistic universe, where the divine life force and every living thing in existence are indivisible. Moore has no issues with the Creator – it's the 'Middle Management' that he objects to. In Moore's popcorn philosophy, God is akin to Elvis and religious authorities are all clones of Colonel Tom Parker, marketing his property to those starving for spiritual sustenance.

Many might consider that it takes more than a leap of faith to connect comic books and pop culture with occultism but, as Moore observes, the graphic nature of comics seems to stimulate the right-hand hemisphere of the brain, the side that relates to the imagination or the underworld of the unconscious.

Moore Magic

His distrust of organized religion aside, Moore acknowledges that Judaeo-Christian symbology and concepts are crucial to magical thought and he has admitted that his own workings have touched upon some of these areas 'with a fierce intensity'. One of these rites involved a vision of the Mysteries of the Crucifixion.

'... and it goes without saying that something like that certainly leaves an impression. I would imagine that my personal notion of Jesus is possibly a great deal more immediate and real than that of a great many people who would profess to be practising Christians.'

In Moore's opinion the various religions can be compared to the languages of the world, each expressing the same ideas in a different form, while magic can be likened to linguistics, the science of language.

Magic, according to Moore, is not a ticket to an alien environment, but a new way of seeing the world around us, a different way of perceiving what the rest of us take for granted.

'I've heard it said that all of our human perceptions might be seen as our individual windows on the Universe. The magician is con-

sciously attempting to alter his or her window's width or its angle, so as to get a different view of the landscape outside. The schizo-phrenic, on the other hand, has had his or her window kicked in by some great big astral skinhead in eighteen-hole Doctor Martens boots. Both of them are experiencing the same flood of phenomena and probably many of the same perceptions. The magician, howev-er, has a means of processing this information.'

He likens magical consciousness, the altered state of heightened awareness, to a musical fugue in which many melodic lines are played simultaneously. The listener can choose which strand to focus upon, or simply allow the counterpoint to wash over them, although he admits that during a magical operation the images and sensations are not always as harmonious, nor as uplifting as the musical variety. It is more likely to be 'disorienting, overwhelming, even terrifying'.

'I suppose I'd have to say that for anyone who has had or believes themselves to have had an extra normal experience, a reaction of pants-shitting holy terror is only to be expected, as are all sorts of confused and meaningless spiritual anxiety dredged up from what-ever vestigial religious upbringing we went through or whatever hysterical Dennis Wheatley occult novels we happened to read dur-ing our formative years ... The further I explore these ideas, howev-er, the more it seems to become apparent that concepts like "good" or "evil" mean absolutely nothing above a certain fundamental hu-man level. A bit higher up still and even things like individual con-sciousness have no meaning ... The entities which we traditionally think of as "other" are in a sense nothing but ourselves unfolded – or at a higher frequency.'

THEY SOLD THEIR SOULS FOR ROCK AND ROLL

'A little knowledge is a dangerous thing.'

Anon

The record labels of mainstream Heavy Metal bands are putting increasing pressure on their groups to exorcize their black magic image, which now appears contrived and clichéd in comparison to the new generation of hardcore Black Metal bands, who play harder and faster than their aging predecessors. Pressure from parental lobby groups and Christian activists has forced the record companies to persuade many bands to tone down their occult obsessions and distance themselves from the truly Satanic legions who proudly boast of their allegiance to the dark side. But is there more to this mass exorcism than a desperate attempt to stall declining sales? Do any of the bands really believe in the Black Arts, or is it simply an act? And is there any real danger in worshipping at the altar of the metal gods?

Alice Cooper, godfather of Goth rock and one-time purveyor of the most perversely pleasurable stage show on the planet, considers Marilyn Manson and the nu-metal merchants to be his 'disobedient children', not the acolytes of the Antichrist that they claim to be. For Alice and his contemporaries – Ozzy Osbourne, Judas Priest, Kiss, Twisted Sister, Mötley Crüe, et al. – the Satanic symbolism, sado-masochistic accessories and on-stage violence that made them every parent's nightmare in the 1970s and 1980s were merely theatrical trappings designed to create a provocative and enduring image.

In real life Alice (who was given his stage name by a Ouija board) reads his Bible every day like the God-fearing son of a preacher man that he is and Ozzy has become the nation's favourite eccentric uncle as he shuffles through his Hollywood mansion in carpet slippers, struggling to cope with modern technology on *The Osbournes*, a reality TV show. Being a working-class lad from Birmingham, Ozzy has always had his tongue firmly wedged in his cheek, except of course when he was biting the heads off bats. But once viewers had witnessed him struggling with a TV remote and taking lip from his kids, he no longer seemed like a threat to the nation's youth. As for his carefully-cultivated image as the Crown Prince of Darkness, he now admits that the members of Black Sabbath were so shaken after watching *The Exorcist* that they had to sleep in the same bed.

'That's how Satanic we were!'

Only Make-believe

Rock music is all about image and style. The band with the strongest image and the most distinctive style has the best chance of standing apart from the pack. Had Kiss not come up with their pantomime make-up it is doubtful whether their music would have brought them the stardom they craved. Satanic symbolism is one of the strongest and most indelible images in our culture, so it is no surprise that numerous bands have seized upon it as a way of getting a ready and eager audience to follow them down the highway to hell and beyond. However, many of these bands might be virulently anti-Christian but they are not true Satanists. They use Satanic symbolism in their artwork, and they quote Lovecraft, Crowley and LaVey in their lyrics, just as punk bands used the swastika to provoke a reaction and draw attention to themselves.

Nevertheless, a small minority of bands fervently believe that the devil has all the best tunes and that the only way to survive in a violent world is to align oneself with the Lords of Chaos. In Scandinavia, the Black Metal movement has spawned extremists, who have been accused of burning churches to the ground and even committing murder. But these crimes come from the perpetrators' pre-existing psychoses, not from music – no matter how manic and aggressive it might be.

THE DEVIL'S MUSIC

'You must have the devil in you to succeed in any of the arts.'

Voltaire

Music is the medium through which our souls can sing or howl in pain. It can both soothe the savage breast and arouse the passions. The earliest songs celebrated the intoxicating power of wine and the bitter sweet highs and lows of love. Even the early monastic liturgies often had an earthy, secular theme (such as the medieval Latin verses that were set to music by 20th-century composer Carl Orff, whose oratorio *Carmina Burana* became a proto-metal anthem). And long before punk rock gave the finger to the Establishment, balladeers entertained villagers with lusty airs. In the 20th century, jazz was condemned for inciting lewd and lascivious acts, though it is now seen as the height of sophistication. And then came the blues.

The devil presided at the birth of the blues in the Mississippi Delta in the 1920s and he has kept a tight grip on his wanton off-spring ever since. It was not just the fact that blues singers were black and were therefore considered a threat to their white masters in the segregated southern United States, even after the abolition of slavery. No, it was the fact that the black man and his kin were determined to enjoy what little life had to offer them and that often meant dancing, drinking, music and sex, with maybe a little dice and dope on the side. But there was another, rarely acknowledged, reason why polite white society and the Church authorities were suspicious, even fearful, of black music. The blues sounded other-worldly to white folks and it smacked of voodoo and the mysteries of the 'dark continent'. That was because it diverted from the conventional chromatic music scale by flattening the seventh note. The 'blues scale' was therefore the direct descendant of the 'Devil's Trill', which the medieval Church had deemed unnatural and therefore unholy. What more proof was needed that the blues was indeed the devil's music?

DOWN TO THE CROSSROADS

'I don't give the devil credit for creating nothing.'

Little Richard

One of the most enduring legends in rock's brief but turbulent history tells how Robert Johnson, 'King of the Delta Blues Singers', sold his soul to the devil at the crossroads on Highway 61 at midnight, in return for some cool licks and a fistful of neat tunes. An awkward youth, he had been booed off stage only nine months earlier and so when he returned to play the Delta juke joints after making his pact with the Prince of Darkness, the crowd was spooked by the transformation. His fame spread faster than a forest fire, but at night Johnson was haunted by dreams in which the devil pursued him down a long dirt road to the boneyard. These nightmares inspired classic songs such as 'Crossroad Blues', 'Me And the Devil Blues' and 'Hellhound On My Trail', which have since become a staple of the blues and rock repertoire. The devil cashed in his chit early, however. Johnson was apparently poisoned by a club owner, who suspected the singer of seducing his wife. He died foaming at the mouth and was buried in an unmarked grave by the locals, who refused to lay him in consecrated ground for fear the devil would come to claim his own. A more prosaic explanation for Johnson's miraculous gifts is that he was taken under the wing of local bluesman Ike Zinneman, who had a habit of haunting graveyards, where he could practise in peace. But if the legend sounds better than the facts, then the legend must stand.

When the blues artists left their rural backwaters for Chicago, in search of record contracts and a regular gig, they soon found that they needed to amplify their guitars if they were to be heard above the rattle of the L-trains and the constant traffic noise. Electric guitars, bass, drums and miked vocals made for a raunchier, rhythm-driven sound and with it more earthy lyrics, which only enhanced the music's reputation for promoting debauchery and drugs. But the Church did not come out in force against the new 'race' music until it threatened to 'corrupt' a white audience through the high priests of rock and roll – Elvis Presley, Jerry Lee Lewis, Chuck Berry and Little Richard. As soon as rock was unleashed upon a generation of teenagers who had never had a voice before, it was condemned from the pulpit as 'jungle music' and society blamed it for the subsequent rise in drunkenness, vandalism and violence. Rock and the devil have been inseparable ever since.

LET IT BLEED

'Gossip is the devil's radio.'

George Harrison

The primitive 'beat combos' of the early Sixties were no threat to anyone with their anaemic white bubblegum pop, but they soon gave way to the psychedelic movement, whose foremost exponents

The Rolling Stones perform 'Sympathy for the Devil' on stage at the Palais de Sports, Paris, 1970.

experimented with mind-altering substances and promoted exotic philosophies of the East as the way to Nirvana. Rock was getting interesting again.

Even their Satanic majesties The Rolling Stones tuned in and tripped out on acid until they realized that it made their music soft and self-indulgent. So they discarded their kaftans and beads and came up with 'Sympathy for the Devil', the first explicitly Satanic song in the catalogue. They were inspired by the media's self-righteous rage surrounding Anton LaVey's newly-founded Church of Satan. Satanism was a fashionable indulgence for the Stones and many of their followers, like meditation and a pilgrimage to Marrakesh. In 1969 Jagger had collaborated with Californian underground film maker Kenneth Anger on an 11-minute cult movie, *Invocation of My Demon Brother*, which included footage of the cast smoking hashish from a skull and conducting a Satanic funeral for a dead dog. Anger was an avowed disciple of Aleister Crowley and a close friend of Anton LaVey of the Church of Satan. He went on to collaborate with another Crowley acolyte Jimmy Page of Led Zeppelin on a second film, *Lucifer Rising*, in 1972.

It was the press who dubbed Jagger the 'Lucifer of Rock' and the 'unholy roller', but the singer-satyr was only expressing incredulity when he observed, 'There are black magicians who think we are acting as unknown agents of Lucifer.'

The Stones were more interested in sex, drugs and rock and roll than dancing with Mr D, if it required self-discipline and dedication. Their corrupted choirboy persona was merely a cool marketing image. But even evoking such an image could prove fatal. At the Altamont Festival in 1969 a group of Hell's Angels stabbed a fan to death in front of the stage as Jagger performed 'Under My Thumb'. Shocked by the event he unceremoniously dropped the Satanic act and the Stones became a multi-million dollar corporate cabaret act and a harmless parody of their former rebellious selves.

COVEN

Other 'underground' bands, however, found the imagery too tempting to resist and as the hippie dream darkened in the late Sixties, bands such as Black Widow and Coven summoned the faithful to the sabbat. Though strictly second division, Chicago's Coven can lay claim to being the first overtly Satanic band to release an album. The closing track of *Witchcraft Destroys Minds and Reaps Souls* is a 13-minute Black Mass which uses a Latin text that the sleeve notes claim is entirely authentic. But even more spooky than the music is the fact that Coven featured a member by the name of Oz Osbourne, who was no relation to England's Ozzy Osbourne, and the same album featured a song with the title 'Black Sabbath'. Maybe the devil has a sense of irony after all. The cover of Coven's 1969 debut also featured what might have been the first appearance of the 'devil's sign', a hand gesture that was later popularized by the late Ronnie James Dio – who replaced Ozzy Osbourne in Black Sabbath. He claimed that he learnt the sign from his Italian grandmother, who told him that it was a traditional protection against 'the evil eye'. The gesture was subsequently used en masse by metal fans, as a way of showing allegiance to their idols. Incidentally, Dio also fronted Ritchie Blackmore's Rainbow, another mainstream rock band with a passing interest in the occult.

Black Widow's debut album, *Sacrifice*, also featured several songs with Satanic themes, among them 'Conjuration', 'Come To The Sabbat' and the title track. Their stage act featured a faux ritual complete with a nude female dancer, which they claimed had been choreographed by Alex Sanders, self-proclaimed 'King of the Witches', but the music was too unremarkable to make a lasting impression.

COME TO THE SABBAT

In contrast, British metal masters Black Sabbath embraced the 'schlock horror' aspect of witchcraft and devil worship wholeheartedly. They named themselves after a stylish Italian horror movie starring Boris Karloff and they served up ripe slices of prime Hammer horror on such brain-bludgeoning tracks as 'The Wizard', 'Children of the Grave', 'War Pigs' and 'Paranoid'.

But the group soon realized that they had prised open a whole can of worms that couldn't be resealed. Fans began reading invocations to Satan into every lyric. 'N.I.B.', for example, was interpreted as an acronym for 'Nativity In Black', but it had in fact been a reference to the drummer's nickname, Nibby. The negative attention they attracted from seriously disturbed fans led to the group writing songs with explicit warnings against dabbling in the occult. They later admitted that they had been uncomfortable with the subject from the start.

In 1966 bassist Geezer Butler was attracted by the occult underground scene, to the extent that he began reading black magic magazines and devouring Dennis Wheatley novels. Having been brought up as a Catholic, he believed in the existence of the devil and so when he began to have precognitive dreams he wondered if these had been sent by the Evil One.

'I had been having loads of these (psychic) experiences since I was a child and finally I was reading stuff that was explaining them. It led me into reading about the whole thing – black magic, white magic, every sort of magic. It's an incredibly interesting subject. I sort of got more into the black side of it and was putting upside down crosses on my wall and pictures of Satan all over. I painted my apartment black. I was getting really involved in it and all these horrible things started happening to me.'

One of Geezer's most disturbing supernatural experiences inspired the title track from the band's eponymous debut album, which helped to launch their 40-year career. He had been lying in bed one night after reading a book on the occult given to him by Ozzy when he sensed a malign presence. When he opened his eyes he was terrified to see a large black shape like a monk standing at the end of the bed. Its face was hidden by a cowl. After a moment or two it disappeared, but its malign aura remained like a pungent aroma. The next morning Geezer discovered that the book had gone. He 'knew' intuitively that the thing, whatever it was, had been drawn by the book and he swore never to read anything on the subject again.

'I saw it as a sign that I needed to either get in all the way or get out completely. I chose to get out!'

Unfortunately, the band's most ardent disciples were not so easily expelled. One group of devotees camped outside their hotel room and performed an improvised Black Mass, which Ozzy, Bill, Tony and Geezer ruined by singing 'Happy Birthday' and blowing out their black candles.

STAIRWAY TO HELL

Black Sabbath never scaled the heights of their rivals Led Zeppelin during their initial run, but then Zeppelin had the assistance of a shadowy figure who made concert promoters and record labels an offer they didn't dare to refuse. And I am not referring to their intimidating manager Peter Grant. No. Zeppelin were said to have entered into a pact with Lucifer himself in exchange for fame. Well, whether or not there is any truth to that, it is a matter of record that after scoring a string of platinum albums and record-breaking concert tours the band suffered a number of personal tragedies, which culminated in the death of drummer John Bonham and their decision to call it a day. Rock scribes and superstitious fans who had bought into the whole occult myth blamed it all on the curse of Aleister Crowley, with whom Page was obsessed. Page had purchased Boleskin House, near Loch Ness, the home of the notorious magician, and he owned a priceless collection of Crowley manuscripts and first editions, which was said to be one of the finest in the world. Page explained his obsession with Crowley during an interview.

'I feel Aleister Crowley is a misunderstood genius of the 20th century. Because his whole thing was liberation of the person,

of the entity, and that restrictions would foul you up ... He was a master of evil but you can't ignore evil if you study the supernatural as I do ... I think Crowley is completely relevant to today ... Magic is very important if people can go through with it.'

When asked by *Guitar World* magazine in 2008 how intense his interest was in the occult, Page replied, 'I was living it. That's all there is to it. It was my life – that fusion of magick and music.'

Sigils and Symbols

Page confirmed that the sigils (occult symbols) featured on the *Led Zeppelin IV* album cover and the embroidered designs on his stage clothes were not mere decorations but expressions of talismanic magic. His 'Zoso' symbol was a combination of astrological signs taken from a 16th-century alchemical grimoire, *Ars Magica Arteficii*, and his 'Dragon Suit' was embroidered with the symbols for Capricorn, Scorpio and Cancer, which are his Sun, Ascendant and Moon signs.

'Yes, I knew what I was doing. There's no point in saying much about it, because the more you discuss it, the more eccentric you appear to be. But the fact is – as far as I was concerned – it was working, so I used it ... I'll leave this subject by saying the four musical elements of Led Zeppelin making a fifth is magick into itself. That's the alchemical process.'

In the early 1970s Page owned an occult bookshop and publishing house, The Equinox Booksellers and Publishers, in London's Kensington High Street, but he sold it once Zeppelin took off and his family life became more demanding. However, his interest in the occult never waned and with the royalties from record sales and concert tours he was able to send his personal assistants out to scour antiquarian bookshops for rare occult manuscripts and first editions.

Zeppelin's albums only contain fleeting, obscure references to the occult, however, and even these are ambiguous and open to interpretation. Page might have been under Crowley's spell but he was astute enough to realise that overt references to magic would only appeal to a minority.

NWOBHM

The 1980s saw the likes of Zeppelin and the other dinosaurs of rock toppled from their pedestals by NWOBHM (not a mythical Nordic god but a contraction of the New Wave of British Heavy Metal), which was spearheaded by a brood of snotty young upstarts who found the ponderous riffs of yore too slow and the tunes too er ... tuneful. Enter Black Metal and its bastard brethren Death Metal, Thrash Metal, Prog Metal, Symphonic Metal and the ultimate sin, Folk Metal – played so fast that if they printed the score it would be a burnt black streak across the page. The vocals were an unintelligible growl like the birth pangs of a wounded werewolf and the drummers needed the stamina and speed of an Olympic sprinter to sustain the double bass pedals at cardiac arrest tempo. Such was the unholy sound of Acheron, Angel Witch, Anaal Nathrakh, Bathory, Cloven Hoof, Cradle of Filth, December Moon, Ewigkeit, Hecate, Hell Satan, King Diamond (aka Mercyful Fate), Lord Belial, Meads Of Asphodel, Megiddo Bal Sagoth, Onslaught, Pagan Altar, Reign Of Erebus, Sabbat, Venom, Warhammer and Witchfynde, to name just a few of the legions of the damned.

This was not music, it was war. The apocalypse was upon us.

Venom declared, 'We are not here to entertain you but to preach the ways of Satan.' Their manifesto was made plain in the song 'Possessed' which states, 'I am possessed by all that is evil. The death of your God I demand. I ... sit at Lord Satan's right hand.'

But what their critics failed to take into account was that artists sing 'in character'. Their lyrics do not always represent their personal beliefs or feelings. Did Arthur Brown really believe he was a fire demon when he sang 'I am the God of hellfire'? Hell no. Did Jagger think he was Lucifer incarnate when he asked for sympathy for the old devil? No. He was acting the part for the sake of a song. And when Vincent Damon Furnier beheaded dolls and sang 'No More Mr Nice Guy' he did so as his alter ego and stage persona, Alice Cooper, entertainer. Only someone who believes that rock is the devil's music would assume that the spirit that inspires and moves an artist in mysterious ways is anything other than their muse.

That said, some of the Black Metal merchants took themselves very seriously indeed. Acheron went one better than the rest by recruiting Peter Gilmore from the Church of Satan to act as master of ceremonies on their album *The Rites of the Black Mass*, which contained the lines 'Glory to thee almighty Satan ... Thou art lord, thou alone, oh mighty Satan'. Morbid Angel boasted that they were 'Satan's sword' on a mission to 'rid the world of the Nazarene' and frontman Trey Azagthoth claimed to be a genuine vampire. He proved it by biting himself on stage and drinking his own blood. Showmanship or insanity? Who can say. Only a qualified shrink, perhaps. In the words of 'In Conspiracy With Satan', by Bathory, 'The lies of Christ will lose, the ways of hell I chose.'

And then there were bands on the fringes of punk, Goth rock and other genres, who also professed to have Satanic sympathies, namely Skinny Puppy, Flesheaters, Diamanda Galas, Christian Death, Current 93 and Psychic TV, whose founders were active occultists.

'IN LORD SATAN WE TRUST' – SLAYER

Many of the nu generation came and went as swiftly as a bolt from Thor's fingertips, but for a few short years they were worshipped by seething hordes of leather-clad acolytes, who gathered in the shadow of monolithic Marshall stacks (music amplifiers) wreathed in dry ice to pay homage to their metal gods. Possessed by the dark spirit of the power chord they writhed as uninhibited as any tribal shaman to the accompaniment of bone-crunching riffs and rib-rattling screams that could have summoned the beast from the pit. These concerts were pagan rites of passage in all but name. As guitarist Craig Chaquico of AOR (adult-oriented rock) act Jefferson Starship observed, 'Rock concerts are the churches of today.'

Had the bands been serious practitioners of the Black Arts who knows what forces they might have unleashed? Instead they came, they sweated and they sold a lot of merchandise. But not one of them succeeded in conjuring a demon unless it was the demon alcohol. Even violence was minimal at the majority of these modern Dionysian rites. Had there been any serious intent to invoke evil, 10,000 watts of electric power and thousands of headbangers whipped to a frenzy would have done it.

And yet the mere presence of pentagrams on record sleeves and the number 666 on T-shirts was sufficient to give the moral minority apoplexy. Nikki Sixx of Mötley Crüe explained to a *Rock Beat* reporter how the Satanic imagery can become twisted by those who miss the irony.

'On the second album, we told them to "Shout at the Devil". A lot of people ... think that song is about Satan. That's not true. It's about

standing up to authority, whether it is your parents, your teacher or your boss. That is pretty good advice, I think. But I'm sure that any parent who hears it is going to think it is treason.'

In 1984 he made a confession to *Circus* magazine.

'We have skulls, pentagrams, and all kinds of Satanic symbols on stage ... I've always flirted with the devil.'

Peter Criss, the drummer with Kiss, whose worst sin was to infringe the rules of good taste, did his best to sound sinister when he said:

'I believe in the Devil as much as I believe in God. You can use either one to get things done.'

PLAY IT LOUD ...
AND BACKWARDS

'You know what you get when you play Twisted Sister's "Burn in Hell" backwards? "Go to church and pray on Sunday".'

Jay Leno (comedian)

By the mid-1980s occult symbols and Satanic song titles were proliferating faster than Gideon Bibles. Every metal band seemed to be labouring under the impression that having a pentagram on the cover of their album, or the number of the beast in a lyric, was a more effective marketing gimmick than posing with a naked model in leather and chains. As the bands became more outrageous in their open celebration of Satanic imagery, so the moral majority became increasingly indignant about what they saw as their insidious influence on their impressionable fans. Finally, the righteous could repress their rage no longer. They launched an aggressive campaign against several iconic rock acts, who were accused of including subliminal Satanic messages in their music. These messages were said to be audible only when the music was played backwards, a feat that was no longer possible in the CD era. Grieving families who had lost their teenage sons to suicide were encouraged to sue the boys' favourite artists, on the grounds that they had incited the youngsters to take their own lives by encoding these messages in their music, a technique known as backward masking.

Suicide Call

In October 1984, 19-year-old John McCollum shot himself in the head with a.22 calibre handgun after listening to a number of Ozzy Osbourne albums, including *Blizzard of Oz*, which features the song 'Suicide Solution'. When police arrived at the scene they found the teenager still wearing headphones, with the smoking gun at his side, which suggested that his death was spontaneous and had a direct link with the music he was listening to at the time. It was said that the boy had been suffering from depression and had an alcohol problem. Grief-stricken and incensed at what they believed to be the rock star's irresponsible and reckless indifference to the tragedy, McCollum's parents instigated legal proceedings against the singer and his label CBS. It was just one of the three lawsuits that Ozzy was forced to defend at that time.

Two other teenagers had killed themselves in similar circumstances, while allegedly under the influence of his Satanic spell. When the McCollum case came to trial in California in January 1986, the slavering media saw it as a critical test case.

Dressed conservatively in a tailored suit that would have put a Bible-thumping evangelist to shame, Ozzy took the stand to protest that the song was in fact inspired by his own self-destructive drinking habit and was intended as a warning against over-indulgence and self-abuse. The word 'solution' in the title, he said, referred to alcohol, not a drastic answer to one's personal problems. Alcoholism was a form of suicide.

Furthermore, Ozzy argued, his image as the devil-worshipping Prince of Darkness was all part of his act. He had no agenda to convert the nation's youth to Satanism. Rock was entertainment, nothing more. Unimpressed, the prosecution alleged that Ozzy had hidden subliminal messages in an instrumental section of the song, which encouraged listeners to 'Get the gun – shoot', a suggestion the singer strenuously denied.

Under pressure by the relentless questioning, Ozzy spat: 'I swear on my kid's life I never said "get the fucking gun".'

Devil's Advocate

Neither the judge nor the jury could make out what was being said in the offending passage, which was totally obscured by the screaming guitar feedback, the rumbling bass and the thundering drums, so they turned to the experts from the Institute for Bio-Acoustics Research to play devil's advocate. The IBAR boffins subjected 'Suicide Solution' to intense scrutiny in their laboratory, filtering it through state-of-the-art sound equipment to isolate the madman's incoherent mumblings, which they claimed had been recorded at one and a half times the normal rate of speech, presumably to avoid detection by the casual listener.

Their report concluded that the 'meaning and true intent' of the subliminal lyrics, 'becomes clear after being listened to over and over again'. The offending lines were said to be 'Why try, why try? Get the gun and try it! Shoot, Shoot, Shoot', followed by a demonic laugh. Anticipating the argument that the defence might offer, that these words were ad-libs, the scientific experts revealed that they had identified something far more sinister in the track. The presence of Hemi-Sync® tones had been detected. These high frequency signals are a patented process that was developed to aid the assimilation of information by the human brain. They could not have been incorporated into the recording accidentally.

This was disputed by the defence, who argued that Ozzy had been messing around at the mixing desk, so the so-called lyrics were a mere sound effect. Besides, he was free under the First Amendment to the US Constitution to write and record anything he wished, unencumbered by the worry that someone might misinterpret what he had said.

The judge agreed.

'Musical lyrics and poetry cannot be construed to contain the requisite "call to action" for the elementary reason they simply are not intended to be and should not be read literally ... Reasonable persons understand musical lyrics and poetic conventions as the figurative expressions which they are.'

And the court of appeal concurred that the devil might have all the best tunes, but if his lyrics are unintelligible there is no risk to his fans.

Ozzy Osbourne's acquittal did not stop a civil action being brought against Judas Priest in 1990. According to the prosecution, 20-year-old James Vance and 18-year-old Raymond Belknap attempted to end their lives with a shotgun after listening to Judas Priest music. Belknap was successful but Vance only managed to blow part of his face away.

When the case came to court in Nevada, part of the prosecution's case was that one of the band's songs contained the command 'do it' when it was played backwards. The band's defence team responded by demonstrating that the same song, again played backwards, also contained the totally harmless message, 'I asked for a peppermint, I asked her to get one.'

At the end of the trial the judge dismissed the case. He told the court that when speech is played backwards those who wish to hear intelligible phrases will interpret the garbled sounds as such, but that is unintentional on the part of the artist. In consequence, no artist can be held responsible for what their listeners might hear or do when in a disturbed state of mind.

SATANIC ROCK ROLLS ON

'The devil's voice is sweet to hear.'

Stephen King (horror writer)

By the beginning of the 1990s most of the NWOBHM bands, and the first generation of Black Metal gods, were history, having split or been sidelined by the next big thing. Their demise was no doubt hastened by the Satanic ritual abuse scandal which tainted bands by association, even those who protested that it was all just an act. However, after the dust had settled Satanic rock rose louder and prouder than ever in the form of Mötley Crüe, Marilyn Manson, Deicide, Slipknot, Rob Zombie, Slayer and a resurrected Ozzy Osbourne, whose MTV reality show had made him bigger than ever. He was too cherished a 'character' to be demonized by the moral minority.

Not all self-confessed Satanists were Black Metal merchants. Marilyn Manson dresses his message in a hybrid of Glam Metal to make it MTV friendly – though he was reputedly 'ordained' as a priest in the Church of Satan and at one time tore Bibles to pieces on stage.

In August 1996 he confided his aspirations to *Spin* magazine.

'Hopefully, I'll be remembered as the person who brought an end to Christianity.'

And in October of the same year he told *Hit Parader* (p.28) how he was going to do it.

'I don't know if anyone has really understood what we're trying to do. This isn't just about shock value … that's just there to lure the people in. Once we've got 'em we can give 'em our MESSAGE.'

Manson's passion for LaVey's amoral philosophy began at an early age, if we are to believe his 'confessions'.

'My mom used to tell me when I was a kid, "If you curse at night time, the devil's going to come to you when you're sleeping". I used to get excited because I really wanted it to happen … I wanted it. I wanted it more than anything …'

(*Rolling Stone*, January 1997)

All Part of the Act

But for the majority of bands Satanism is all part of the branding and marketing of their music. If the Satanic bands were true believers they would adhere to the credo of the magus, which is 'to dare, to will, to know and to be silent'. No true magician, black or white, would publicize his methods or indulge in self-promotion, for to do so is to attract attention to what should be a private act of devotion. Success in the art of magic depends upon the ability to focus the will on that which you wish to bring into being. The attention of outsiders would be an unwelcome distraction.

By sensationalizing and over-simplifying occult practices the so-called Satanic bands, and others who flirt with superficial Satanic symbols, add to the smokescreen of myth and misunderstanding. Real magic requires dedication, self-discipline and serious study. Nothing of real value or insight can come to those who purchase their powers over the counter. A quick fix only brings trouble. As author Dennis Wheatley once warned, 'one does not have to know the secret rituals to attract the powers of darkness'.

The Buck Stops Here

Kevin Carlyon is a white witch and the author of a number of books on the occult. He told this author that he believes that anyone who exploits Satanic themes for profit or sells them as harmless entertainment should take responsibility for encouraging an unhealthy interest in the dark side of our psyche.

'Most of the members of our coven and other people I have met over the years who practise magic seem to have become involved initially through rock music. Many are bikers or heavy rock fans whose interest in the occult was aroused by the symbols on the record sleeves or by references in the lyrics. It's not important whether the bands themselves believe in what they are singing about or not. If their followers see these symbols on the album covers they naturally assume that there must be something of substance behind it.

'The first rule of magic is to put an intention in the mind of the person you are trying to influence, just as voodoo priests send advance warnings to their victims. From Egyptian times certain beats and sounds have been used to put the subject into a trance-like state, in which the mind is susceptible to suggestion. Ozzy

Osbourne and other artists may deny the existence of the devil, but their music still exerts a strong influence on those who are open to it. Some rock lyrics are like chants or mantras. They can release a dark memory to trouble or obsess the mind, especially if the powers of reason are weakened by drugs or alcohol. These subliminal messages can then come across as definite commands to the suggestible individual.

'A fundamental rule of magic is that if you believe in what you are repeating then it will cause things to occur, if only in your mind. Sometimes we make up our own spells for special situations, but we believe they work because we believe in the force behind them. Conversely, people can convince themselves that they are possessed and to all intents and purposes they are, but not by a separate conscious malign entity. They will have allowed their own fears to take over. We maintain that there is a dark psyche in everyone and that our thoughts encourage one side or the other to dominate at any given time. In feeding your mind on Satanic doctrine you are raising your own personal demon to torment you.'

THE SATANIC PANIC

'People who cease to believe in God or goodness altogether still believe in the devil. I don't know why. No, I do indeed know why. Evil is always possible. And goodness is eternally difficult.'

Anne Rice (author)

During the seismic social and cultural revolution of the 1960s, members of the religious right in Europe and the United States feared they were being overwhelmed by a wave of secularism that would drown out their shrill self-righteous protests and sweep them back to the Dark Ages. If only they could find evidence that Satan was the real architect of the permissive society, the corrupter of youth, the mastermind behind the illegal drug cartels and the sinister puppet master behind the 'degenerate' entertainment industry.

So desperate were they to find something that would justify their collective paranoia that they eagerly embraced the Satanic conspiracy theory without pausing to question its veracity or to consider the consequences.

SATAN IN SUBURBIA

In 1980 American psychiatrist Dr Lawrence Pazder published an account of a controversial new therapeutic technique, which he claimed had been used to recover suppressed 'memories' from a patient who had suffered abuse at the hands of a Satanic cult. When Michelle Smith sought treatment for psychological problems for which she had no explanation, Dr Pazder volunteered to probe her unconscious by means of Recovered Memory Therapy (RMT).

Under hypnosis, Smith 'recalled' being forced to participate in ritual sacrifices, in which she drank blood and was abused by the devil himself while her parents watched. Pazder was so elated by his success that he did not consider that these graphic incidents might be delusions – symptoms of a neurosis that could be treated with more conventional methods. Before the technique and his findings could be properly evaluated, Pazder rushed to publish a book, *Michelle Remembers*, which became an instant best-seller and the hottest talk show topic in town.

The situation was immediately seized upon by the religious right. Here was proof at last that the devil and his legions were up to their old tricks once again. Michelle was honoured by the Vatican as a 'Satanic survivor', the first of many to come forward once the promise of publicity and celebrity beckoned. Meanwhile, the good doctor and his patient divorced their respective partners and were married.

Bearing False Witness

Repressed memories formed the basis of a slew of similar books such as *Satan's Underground* by Lauren Stratford and *He Came to Set the Captives Free* by Rebecca Brown, whose revelations of alleged systematic Satanic child abuse generated an entire new genre known as 'Satanic survival'. In the white heat of hysteria that followed these publications, no one thought to ask why earlier cases of ritual abuse had not come to light. Before reason could prevail, the flames of moral indignation were fanned once again when a former member of a Satanic cult, Mike Warnke, offered to expose the crimes that had been committed in the name of Satan. By doing so he became an instant celebrity on the chat show circuit.

Warnke claimed to have been a high priest of Satan in San Bernardino, California. He had attempted to profit from his past back in 1972, with the publication of a book called *The Satan Seller*. His disclosures brought him instant notoriety and lucrative speaking engagements on the evangelical revival circuit, but the fees he commanded were chicken feed compared to the millions of dollars he harvested in the wake of the Satanic panic in the 1980s. For the 1980s was the time for revelations. And the more lurid they were, the better. It was also the time for false prophets and unquestioning devotion.

No one questioned Warnke's account of a nationwide occult conspiracy to corrupt children or his claims to have ministered to over 1,500 Satanists in California. His appearances on *Larry King Live* and *The Oprah Winfrey Show* endorsed his reputation as a self-appointed expert on the occult and led to him being invited to act as a consultant to the police, in what appeared to be occult crimes.

But Warnke's life began to unravel in 1991 when the Christian magazine *Cornerstone* published the results of its exhaustive investigations into his lifestyle. (Author's note: *Cornerstone* also investigated numerous allegations of Satanic ritual abuse, including those which had formed the basis of Lauren Stratford and Rebecca Brown's books, and concluded that the charges were unfounded. The magazine investigators accused Stratford of having lied about giving up her newborn child for sacrifice. In fact, they questioned if the baby had ever existed.)

Warnke declared that he had been a long-haired drug-taking Satanist in the late Sixties, but photographs of him taken at the time showed a conventional Mr Average. His claim to have attended a Satanic ritual with Charles Manson on a particular date was also proven false, because Manson was incarcerated at the time and had no affiliations to Satanic organizations. Accounting irregularities, marital scandals and his own begrudging admission to having 'exaggerated' his experiences severely damaged his image. He failed to name one single member of his California coven, which he had dramatically downsized from 1,500 to just 13. Overnight the Christian community turned against him. In 2002 he published a rebuttal, *Friendly Fire: A Recovery Guide for Believers Battered by Religion*, and went on a low-key tour billed as a 'Christian comedian'.

But the laughs were few and far between.

OCCULT CRIMES

'The devil is an optimist if he thinks he can make people worse than they are.'

Karl Kraus (20th-century philosopher)

At one time the devil was thought to be behind every evil act, but nowadays we tend to explain deviant behaviour in more prosaic ways. Crime is seen as a mild form of insanity, a temporary aberration in right-minded people, a lack of empathy or simple selfishness. Blaming the devil for their own actions is the last resort of the criminally insane, although a section of society still attributes the depravity of the worst offenders to the influence of a malevolent entity, in spite of evidence to the contrary. Even minor examples of desecration to churches and graveyards are seen as the work of a Satanic conspiracy, rather than mindless vandalism.

Some religious fundamentalists see the shadow of the devil in every modern activity that they personally disapprove of, from pornography and drug abuse to fortune-telling and New Age complementary therapies. They also call for *The Satanic Bible* to be publicly burned, but the unpalatable fact remains that the majority of ritualistic murders are carried out by killers who find inspiration or justification in the Bible. Does this mean that the Bible too should be banned?

NOT ALWAYS SATAN

As FBI special agent Kenneth V. Lanning observed in a comprehensive report on the subject of Satanic ritual killings in 1992, if a murder is committed during Hallowe'en or on Walpurgis Night why do we assume that it has been committed by Satanists, when a similar homicide attracts no special attention if it is perpetrated on Easter Sunday or Christmas Day? Genuine Satanists do not practise the ritual sacrifice of humans or even animals and they abhor publicity, because they know that persecution will follow. In fact, they do not believe that killing is justified, except in self-defence. And why would God or Satan need to rely on Satanists to do their killing for them, if they are truly omnipotent?

Many teenage dabblers in the occult soon tire of the subject when they realize that sacrificing small animals or vandalizing churches does not bring them what they desire. Those who torture animals in the name of Satan do so because they are mentally disturbed, not because they have a serious interest in Satanism. These individuals eventually end up in mental institutions. Others find other outlets for their extremism. The founder of one Satanic website observed that some teenage Satanists become neo-Nazis while others are attracted to Christian fundamentalist groups.

THE SIGNIFICANCE OF RITUAL

It is misleading to label all ritualistic killings as occult or Satanic. A ritual killing invariably involves a repeated act that satisfies the killer's needs in some way, but it is not to be confused with a sacrificial killing. Killers who violate their victims in a particular way, or who perform some form of ritual act which has a significance for them alone, are fulfilling a fetishistic compulsion, not worshipping the devil. Carving a pentagram on a corpse, or posing the victim to mimic Christ's Crucifixion, might well be part of the killer's signature, but it has no Satanic significance whatsoever.

Criminals may perform rituals while they are committing their crimes because it is a part of their psychosis, or because they imagine that they can hear voices instructing them to do so. Alternatively, the ritualistic aspect of the crime could be there to justify the offence, or it might be a way of alleviating the perpetrator's sense of guilt – such as when a murderer mutilates a victim in order to dehumanize the body. Again, this cannot be interpreted as a Satanic ritual or an occult crime.

Ritualistic abuse is slightly different in that it is often carried out in the name of a traditional religion or a Satanic cult. The malefactor might introduce the ritual aspect simply to intimidate the victim into believing that the act is God's will, or they might be attempting to justify the crime in their own minds. When an unwilling or indoctrinated victim is subjected to abuse it is irrelevant whether the abuser invokes the name of Satan or God to justify his actions. The abuse is a criminal act and the abuser is subject to the penalties prescribed by the law, not the devil.

Long before the subject of occult crime became a regular topic in law enforcement seminars in the United States, Officer Sandi Gallant of the San Francisco Police Department studied the criminal aspects of occult activity and concluded that they provided a rationale for the offender's antisocial behaviour, even though few miscreants held occult beliefs.

Each to His Own

Devil worship and dabbling in the occult might disturb traditional religious groups, who view it as contrary to their own beliefs and values, but interest in the occult is not a crime. Wicca and Satanism are legal forms of worship and their practitioners are equal to followers of other faiths in the eyes of the law, at least in the United States and Western Europe. Offensive though it might be to some, it is a sobering fact that more violent crimes and cases of child abuse have been committed in the name of God than that of the devil. Agent Lanning observed that an adolescent obsession with the occult is usually symptomatic of a psychological problem but it is not the source of it. Hundreds of thousands of people have read *The Satanic Bible* without committing a crime. Millions have listened to Heavy Metal bands and have not been driven to murder. Those who habitually commit serious crimes are clearly predisposed to criminal behaviour and will have cited *The Satanic Bible* or the lyrics of Ozzy Osbourne to absolve themselves of responsibility for their actions.

Many people who hold intense religious beliefs tend to condemn as evil everyone and everything they disapprove of – but the objects of their disapproval often feel the same way about their critics. Evil, like beauty, is in the eye of the beholder, it seems. A religious cult is a Satanic cult in all but name if its members have been conditioned to disown their families, perform acts they would not normally agree to or submit to the will of a charismatic leader.

While any ritual performed in the name of Satan is likely to offend religious individuals, the act itself has to be illegal for a prosecution to be justified. Initiates of Satanism or Wicca point out that orthodox religion encourages practices which those outside that particular belief system may condemn as barbaric. Take for instance circumcision, forcing children to kneel on a stone floor to recite the rosary or the infliction of corporal punishment.

And what of the parents who starve or beat a child because they believe that it is possessed by evil spirits? Or those parents who deny their children medicine because it is forbidden by their religious beliefs? Do we forgive their acts of cruelty or neglect because they are carried out in the name of 'religion' while at the same time prosecuting pagan parents if they adopt similar behaviour? And what of Santeria, the Afro-Caribbean religion that requires the ritual sacrifice of animals and the exorcism of evil spirits? Although animal sacrifices are considered cruel and unnecessary by many non-believers, they were declared constitutional by the US Supreme Court in 1993. It was proven that the killings were for the purposes of initiation and healing and as offerings to the spirits. In the absence of this component the religion would die out.

As Lanning points out, we cannot agree on what Christians believe so why do we assume that all Satanists or Wiccans share identical beliefs? And if one of their kind commits a serious crime such as murder, why presume that their fellow believers will condone it?

What Satanic Murders?

We have seen that the presence of occult symbols at the scene of a murder does not make the crime Satanic. By the same token, a crime that is committed after the perpetrator has read the Bible cannot be dressed up in the cloak of Christianity. It is the individual, not the belief system, who must be held to account.

Genuine Satanic murders are premeditated ritual killings that are committed by individuals whose primary motivation is the sacrifice of their victims. Self-gratification is not a valid criterion, neither is simple bloodlust. After applying this yardstick, Agent Lanning reported that he was unable to identify a single documented case of Satanic murder in the United States.

Lanning concluded his comprehensive report into occult crime with these words.

'After all the hype and hysteria is put aside, the realization sets in that most Satanic/occult activity involves the commission of NO crimes, and that which does usually involves the commission of

relatively minor crimes such as trespassing, vandalism, cruelty to animals, or petty thievery ... as of now there is little or no hard evidence that they (Satanists) are involved in serious, organized criminal activity ... law enforcement is not now locked in a life-and-death struggle against the supernatural forces of ancient evil ... As law enforcement agencies evaluate and decide what they can or should do about Satanic and occult activity in their communities, they might want to also consider how to deal with the hype and hysteria of the "anti-Satanists". The overreaction to the problem can clearly be worse than the problem.'

THE BLACK MAGIC MURDERS OF JACK THE RIPPER

Serial killers and sexual sadists are unfortunately not a modern phenomenon and neither, sadly, are the improbable theories linking many unsolved slayings to the supernatural. The more elusive the killer, it seems, the more fantastic the myth that shrouds the real motive for murder. Without doubt the most morbidly fascinating unsolved case of all is that of Jack the Ripper, who stalked the streets of Whitechapel in 1888. His identity remains unknown to this day. The case is still the subject of intense speculation and it has generated more than its share of fanciful theories, including the idea that the victims were butchered at specific locations as part of an occult ritual.

At the time of the murders, the killer was believed to be a crazed sexual sadist who was hellbent on ridding London's East End of its low-class prostitutes. But why did the murderer's activities stop so suddenly? There are several theories: he was caught and confined to a madhouse; his identity was withheld from the public to spare his family embarrassment; or he committed suicide in a final act of remorse. As early as 1 December 1888 a number

Victorian illustration of Jack the Ripper at work. Was the real murderer an emissary of Satan?'

of conspiracy theories were finding a wide and eager audience, prompted by the publication of an article by occult expert Robert Donston Stephenson in the popular *Pall Mall Gazette*.

The author of the article is now considered to be a prime suspect because his story is seen as evidence of a killer's inability to resist boasting of his crimes.

Stephenson begins by referring his readers to the books of the French magician Eliphas Lévi, who described the means by which it was possible to communicate with the lower spirits and demons and listed the substances that were required to perform the rituals.

'They can only be obtained by means of the most appalling crimes, of which murder and mutilation of the dead are the least heinous. Among them are strips of the skin of a suicide, nails from a murderer's gallows, candles made from human fat, the head of a black cat which has been fed forty days on human flesh, the horns of a goat which has been made the instrument of an infamous capital crime, and a preparation made from a certain portion of the body of a harlot. This last point is insisted upon as essential and it was this extraordinary fact that first drew my attention to the possible connection of the murderer with the black art.'

According to Stephenson it is no coincidence that the six murder sites formed the shape of a cross. (He excluded the seventh victim, Mary Jane Kelly, who was murdered indoors and might therefore not have been killed by the Ripper.) In 2004 statistician Dan Norder analysed the location of the crime scenes for an article in Ripper Notes, the international journal for Jack the Ripper studies, and dismissed Stephenson's black magic theory as statistically unsound.

'When doing calculations of this sort, the size of the number alone in no way proves whether something was random or not. It just proves that there are lots of different possible outcomes ... looking at the map shows that the main roads, although somewhat irregular, mostly form the shape of a cross all by themselves. In other words, most of the features of the patterns people see in the crime scene locations were already present in the layout of the East End before the Ripper killed his first victim.'

Conspiracy theories of this kind also tend to be highly selective, with awkward facts being excluded when they do not conform to the pattern. As well as a cross, the conspiracy theorists attempted to prove that other significant symbols could be formed from an imaginary alignment of the crime scenes. They came up with an arrow pointed towards the Houses of Parliament, a pentacle and a *vesica piscis* (an ancient symbol formed by the intersection of two circles), but in order to make their calculations work they had to exclude some victims who did not fit the pattern and include others who should not really have been there.

Proponents of the arrow theory, for example, exclude victim Catherine Eddowes on the grounds that she might have been murdered by mistake, and replace her with Mary Jane Kelly, ignoring the fact that Kelly was ten years younger and bore no resemblance to Eddowes!

It also needs to be remembered that city maps of the period were notoriously inaccurate and therefore cannot be relied upon to support a theory that centres on the geometrical alignment of specific locations.

But when one is considering the possible occult significance of an unsolved Victorian murder mystery, or a modern Satanic ritual killing, it should be remembered that a madman's motive does not deserve to be taken seriously. It is his crimes that condemn him, not his morbid fantasies.

FOOLS RUSH IN – CHAT SHOW HOSTS GO TO HELL

'The road to hell is paved with good intentions.'

Anon

Popular American TV chat show hosts Oprah Winfrey, Sally Jesse Raphael, Phil Donahue and Geraldo Rivera exert an unprecedented

Chat show host Geraldo Rivera told his audience that there were over a million Satanists in the USA.

influence over their studio audiences and the millions of viewers who watch at home, as do their counterparts in other Western countries. Their opinions are taken as the gospel truth by those who have lost faith in politicians and religious leaders. So it caused a stir when in 1987 Geraldo Rivera told his audience that there were over a million Satanists in the United States. When he went on to say that those same Satanists were suspected of planning 'grisly Satanic murders' and were conspiring to establish a secret underground network for the ritual abuse of children, the nation was shocked and outraged. So incensed were they, in fact, that they tuned in by the million and Rivera's ratings rocketed.

The rival networks could not afford to ignore such a sensational story, so they followed up with exposés of their own, each more lurid than the last. Had Geraldo made such an accusation against any other ethnic or religious group in the United States he would have been denounced and taken off the air, but because his target was Satanism there were few voices raised in protest. Little was known about the Satanists' beliefs but much was assumed, most of it gleaned from low-budget horror movies and the pronouncements made by Heavy Metal bands, who thought the symbolism was cool, but who were as ill-informed as their teenage audience and their parents. It was enough to be told that Satanic sects attracted antisocial types and that their belief system was diametrically opposed to God-fearing Christian family values.

More significantly, few questioned the facts in Geraldo's statement. Had they researched the subject as thoroughly as the chat show host's staff should have done, they would have learnt that the official Satanic churches in the United States could barely muster 10,000 adult members. Another 10,000 or so Satanists practised in private and no more than 100,000 teenagers had fooled around with pseudo-Satanism for a few months before tiring of it when it had failed to bring them results. Few of these people were known to have killed or harmed animals in their rituals. Those who had done so would have been clinically diagnosed as sociopaths, not Satanists.

It was deliberately misleading for Geraldo to suggest that the FBI had the Satanists under surveillance and was anticipating a series of child abductions and ritual killings. The FBI had begun an exhaustive investigation into allegations of organized Satanic or ritual child abuse as far back as 1981, but they had concluded that incidents were isolated and were part of sexual or criminal activity, rather than occult behaviour.

RECOVERED MEMORIES

'It is wonderful how much time good people spend fighting the devil. If they would only expend the same amount of energy loving their fellow men, the devil would die in his own tracks of ennui.'

Helen Keller

(American author and educator, 1880–1968)

The findings of the FBI investigation were not made public at the time of the 'Satanic panic' that had been stirred up by the TV talk shows and even if they had been it was doubtful whether anyone would have accepted them. Middle-and working-class America was seething with righteous indignation and firing itself up for a witchhunt. Hallowe'en parties were banned on suspicion of having been infiltrated by devil worshippers intent on corrupting children and vigilante groups stalked the streets of almost every small town in search of long-haired adolescents with pentagrams or pentacles printed on their T-shirts.

With devil worship and Satanic abuse firmly embedded in the public consciousness, Geraldo hosted a second show in October 1988, in time for Hallowe'en. He invited several self-appointed 'experts' who persuaded Geraldo's viewers that they needed to stamp out this evil before it carried off their sons and daughters. Unknown to their host, however, these experts were not all they claimed to be, if the accusations made against them by evangelical Christian organizations and others are to be believed.

Subsequent shows – the term is used deliberately to emphasize the fact that the purpose of these programmes was for entertainment, not education – explored the highly controversial subject of recovering memories of Satanic and ritual abuse. It was all done with the same highly emotive approach as before. Alleged victims were wheeled on and encouraged to tell their disturbing stories of torture and murder, which they said they had relived during traumatic therapy sessions. Another expert, Dr George K. Ganaway of Emory University, confirmed that the incidence of such memories had reached epidemic proportions. He neglected to add that it was extremely rare to remember events of any kind before the age of three, while memories of childhood prior to the age of two were unknown – yet the majority of quoted cases related to this very period in the victim's life.

Critics of the techniques used in Recovered Memory Therapy (RMT) say that the problem for investigators is that the alleged victims firmly believe that their 'recollections' are real, when it is now suspected that they were inadvertently suggested by the therapist as a possible explanation for the issues that plagued them in adulthood. Dr Ganaway has been quoted as saying that he believed that ill-trained therapists might have been partly responsible for the Satanic abuse scare of the 1980s and 1990s.

Trying to Forget

The case against Recovered Memory Therapy (RMT) crumbled almost overnight when leading mental health specialists began voicing serious doubts about the reliability of the technique, which had never been tested or approved by the profession. This was followed by the collapse of several high profile legal cases, which had relied upon uncorroborated accusations obtained under RMT. Then there was the growing threat of litigation from those who had been falsely accused of Satanic abuse. Further investigations revealed that RMT was scientifically unsound and the results obtained using the technique were highly subjective.

The holy grail of Christian fundamentalism turned into a poisoned chalice as further damage was inflicted on the entire moral crusade when several books on the subject of Satanic ritual abuse were exposed as complete fantasies. No one was denying that children were being abused, but those responsible were not Satanists. Almost a decade after that first sensational exposé, Geraldo Rivera made a public statement in which he apologized for any damage that might have resulted from the hysteria that his show and others like it had whipped up.

'NOW I am convinced that I was terribly wrong ... and many innocent people were convicted and went to prison as a result ... AND I am equally positive [that the] "Repressed Memory Therapy Movement" is also a bunch of CRAP ...'

The hounding of innocent people and the destruction of families by over-zealous social workers, law enforcement personnel and extremist religious groups is as tragic and shameful as the witch trials of the Puritan era and the McCarthy communist witch-hunts of the 1950s. But the most regrettable aspect of the whole sordid affair is that the unjustified moral panic that it caused diverted resources from the victims of real sexual and physical abuse. It is also responsible for the scepticism that now greets each new claim of abuse.

'Religion which requires persecution to sustain it is of the devil's propagation.'

Hosea Ballou

The Thurston County Case

But public apologies were too late for some. Paul Ingram, a law enforcement officer from Thurston County, Washington had been accused of Satanic abuse by his two daughters, after they had viewed one of Geraldo's shows. Both of them had resorted to therapy. In desperation he sought help from his Pentecostal minister, who, it is said, treated the distraught father of three like a criminal. The minister allegedly subjected Ingram to two dozen intense interviews over a five-month period, during which time he was persuaded that Satan can force individuals to commit crimes which are then erased from their memories. Wracked with guilt over what he believed he had done, and fearful of Satan's future influence over him, Ingram apparently confessed – even though there was no physical evidence to corroborate the claims that had been made against him. To date, no other person in the United States has confessed to a charge of Satanic abuse, which gives the lie to the fanciful notion that one million Satanists were conspiring to abduct and abuse children.

But Ingram's confession was false. No crime had been committed. His eldest daughter is said to have claimed that her father had impregnated her and then sacrificed the baby, but a medical examination found no evidence that she had been pregnant. In an attempt to prove how impressionable a suggestible person can be, psychologist Richard Ofshe tried an experiment. He told Ingram that he had forced his son and his daughter to commit incest, a charge Ingram and his children vehemently denied. Then Dr Ofshe asked Ingram to pray for guidance, to see if the 'memory' returned. It did, so Ingram confessed to this 'crime' too. The psychologist then confessed that the crime had never taken place, but Ingram was so indoctrinated with the concept of Repressed Memory Therapy that he could not believe that he was not guilty.

Ingram eventually came to realize that the charges against him were false, so he attempted to change his plea to not guilty. But it was too late. He was sentenced to 20 years in prison.

This is the first and only case to be heard in the United States in which alleged Satanic abuse has been the basis of the charges, although they were dropped at an early stage in favour of rape in the third degree – a fact which speaks volumes for the US judicial system's disdain for the fantasy that is Satanic ritual abuse.

SACRIFICE FOR SATAN

The FBI has officially closed its files on occult killings, having ruled out the possibility that the perpetrators were genuine devil worshippers. Yet there is no denying that in recent years a catalogue of horrific murders in countries as far apart as Argentina, the former Soviet Union and Thailand has been attributed to Satan's servants. But do such diabolical deeds prove that Satan really exists, or is it only that the criminally insane summon him up to serve as a convenient scapegoat for their own aberrant behaviour?

The following cases are habitually cited as proof of the reality of Satanic or occult killings, but this author has researched the background to each crime and has discovered that other factors were present.

- *In July 1970 Steven Hurd and four acolytes were charged in California with two murders involving ritual dismemberment and cannibalism. Hurd later claimed to have licked the blood from the hatchet with which he killed 20-year-old petrol station attendant Jerry Carlin. He also asserted that he ate the heart of*

29-year-old schoolteacher Florence Brown as part of a Satanic initiation ritual. The heart, he said, tasted like chicken. However, Hurd was subsequently diagnosed as insane and his defence attorney has admitted that his client claimed his own father was the devil. There is no forensic evidence to support Hurd's testimony that he ate the victim's heart. The autopsy does not even mention whether the heart or a portion of it was missing. If Hurd had returned to the scene of the crime days later and had then eaten an organ from the decomposing body, as he claimed to have done, it is likely that he would have died or become so seriously ill that his jailers would have reported the fact.

• *In January 1986 Satanic 'priest' Harold Smith and four 'disciples' were jailed for a series of ritual torture-murders in the Rest Haven Cemetery in Houston, Texas. But behind the hysterical headlines the sordid facts of the case revealed that 'High Priest' Smith was a 19-year-old loser who gave himself the title to impress his teenage friends. The cemetery murder was a case of overkill and rage, not ritual. The victim was not ritually slain but brutally assaulted and strangled, leaving him with burnt hair, broken teeth and one eye gouged out of its socket. Two more victims were found shot to death and a third stabbed. A survivor claimed to have been slashed with a knife, but the only occult elements were the choice of murder site and the tattoos on another victim. Smith was declared insane and sentenced to life imprisonment.*

• *In February 1986 self-confessed Crowley disciple Dana Jones, a member of a pseudo sex-magic cult, was arrested for the ritual murder of a man in Denver, Colorado. Acquitted on the grounds of insanity, she escaped from a mental institution in June 1988 and committed suicide. If the cult had been a genuine occult group it would not have admitted someone with serious mental problems.*

- *In September 1987 Ohio Satanist John Fryman was convicted of killing and dismembering 21-year-old Monica Lemen, whose severed legs were disposed of behind an abandoned church. Fryman boasted of having a black-painted ritual chamber in his mobile home, the centrepiece of which was a gravestone he used as an altar. But again, the motive for murder was not magic but jealousy. Fryman shot the woman because he believed she had been unfaithful to him by bringing another 'magician' back to his trailer.*

- *In December 1987 three teenage 'Satanists' in Carl Junction, Missouri – Theron Roland, James Hardy, and Ronald Clements – beat classmate Steven Newberry to death with baseball bats while chanting, 'Sacrifice to Satan!' They had earlier sacrificed animals to their infernal master. As Newberry vainly attempted to fend off the blows he cried out, 'Why are you doing this?' and they shouted, 'Because it's fun'. The jury found them guilty of first-degree murder and the judge sentenced all three to life imprisonment. In a recent television interview Clements admitted that drug abuse had played a part in the killing as well as an obsession with death, which filled the emptiness of their lives. The attack had been spontaneous – it had certainly not been part of a ritual. Asked if he had believed in Satan, as the press had claimed, Clements had to pause and think.*

- *'I don't think that I necessarily wanted to worship Satan ... I don't think that I had a belief in God at that time any more than I had a belief in Satan ... Do I think that I was a Satanist? No, of course not!'*

- *In May 1988 'Satanist' Clifford St Joseph was jailed for having carved an inverted pentagram into his victim's chest during a 'ritual murder', but after an intense investigation of the case FBI special agent Kenneth Lanning concluded that the murder had been nothing more than a sadomasochistic, homosexually-motivated sex crime.*

- *Also in May 1988, American teenage 'Satanist' Terry Belcher boasted of animal sacrifices during his trial for the murder of 15-year-old Theresa Simmons.*

- *'We ate their eyeballs and innards and drank their blood. We toasted the devil by drinking the blood.'*

- *But it was clear from his co-defendants' testimony that the claims were pure fantasy. Simmons had been strangled by Belcher and his two adolescent accomplices after she had refused to have sex with his friend, Robert MacIntyre. They had used a bootlace. Disregarding the claim that it was a ritualistic occultist killing, the judge directed the jury to find the three teenagers guilty of 'malice murder'.*

- *In June 1988 'Satanists' Jason Rose and John Jones videotaped the torture and murder of 19-year-old Melissa Ann Meyer, whom they had asphyxiated by pressing the pole of a spear against her throat. Rune stones and books on occult subjects were found in their possession, but the pair were sadistic thrill-seekers, not*

Satanists. The Lane County police force consulted San Fran-cisco policewoman Sandi Gallant, a specialist on the subject of occult-themed crime, who told them that it appeared that the at-tackers had killed the girl as a human sacri-fice, on the assumption that they would somehow be able to absorb her life force. Deputy District Attorney Brian Barnes was unconvinced.

- *'It turned out to be a mess of belief systems tossed into one very lethal one ... how the heck do you go about selling that to a jury of sensible people?'*

- *In October 1988 22-year-old Joseph Bradsberry was sacrificed by 'California Satanists' Luther Franklin Mays, 19, Wallace Ervin, 23, and Arthur Odell Holley, 26, as part of an initiation ritual. But the Satanic cult headquarters was no more than a basement hangout, where the three teens took LSD, played Dungeons and Dragons and listened to Heavy Metal in the company of their 'ston-er' friends (marijuana smokers). On the night of the murder they watched the horror movie* Evil Dead II *on video and then planned the 'hazing' (humiliation, harassment and abuse) of Bradsberry, which escalated into murder after they handcuffed him. Then they stabbed him in the throat before they beat and drowned him. Their female accomplice reportedly greeted the news of Bradsberry's death with a chillingly matter-of-fact question.*

- *'Well, how did it go? Did he die like a man?'*

- *In September 1990 Daniel Rakowitz, self-styled leader of the Church of 966, was convicted in New York City of the murder of his girlfriend Monika Beerle, whose corpse he had dissected and boiled so that he could carry her skull and bones around in a bucket. The Church of 966 only existed in Daniel's deranged mind, however. As soon as his street friends heard of what he had done to Monika they informed the police, who wisely went along with Daniel's demand to be called the New Messiah, until they had extracted a full confession. Evidently Satan did not take kindly to having his number changed by a drug-addicted disciple who couldn't keep his dastardly deeds to himself.*

- *In July 1991 Michigan 'Satanist' Jaime Rodriguez and his cousin Augustin Pena were convicted and sentenced to life imprisonment for the murder and dismemberment of 15-year-old Stephanie Dubay, a teenage runaway whose severed fingers Rodriguez wore as a charm around his neck. After stabbing the victim ten times in the back and chest, Pena skinned her head and kept her skull in his freezer. According to the medical examiner other body parts had been removed with 'surgical precision' and the body had been subjected to 'meticulous mutilation', which suggests that the motive was pure sadism and not part of a ritual killing. From the books found at their homes, and the substance of their confessions, it was clear that the cousins were dabblers in the occult, but they had no conception of what being a Satanist really entailed. Their world was as crazy as a cartoon in which gratuitous and graphic violence was the principal purpose. The only reason Rodriguez was labelled a Satanist was that the press and the public could not imagine such depravity in a fellow human being unless he had been possessed by the devil.*

- *In December 1992 two 'Satanists' were sentenced to death, and two more were given life imprisonment, for the killing and de-*

capitation of four defectors from their cult in Salida, California. The victims had been hunted down and beaten before being stabbed and decapitated. The episode was designed to serve as a warning to any other cult members who were planning to rebel against their charismatic leader, Gerald Cruz. Cruz used occult dogma, sleep deprivation and electric shocks to keep his followers in line. Cult expert and psychologist Daniel Goldstine considered him to be an 'evil and sadistic' narcissist who would use any means at his disposal to control and condition his weak-willed followers. The group only became 'Satanic' after it had been examined by California's Ritual Crime Investigator's Association, which was looking for proof of Satanic ritual crimes.

- *In April 1994 self-styled Satanist Carey Grayson, 19, abducted, murdered and mutilated a 37-year-old hitchhiker, Vicki DeBlieux, in Alabama after she refused to have sex with him and his three friends – Trace Duncan, 17, Kenny Loggins, 17, and Louis Mangione, 16. Although the press trumpeted the trial as yet another ritualistic occult killing, the medical examiner testified that the victim had been kicked to death in an apparent rage attack and then thrown over a cliff. The mutilations and the possible cannibalism had occurred after the death and so had no ritual significance. The fingers had been removed to make identification difficult and to keep as souvenirs, but Mangione had boasted of the killing to his friends and had shown them the fingers when they had refused to believe his story. Loggins and Grayson were sentenced to death while Mangione and Duncan were given life imprisonment.*

- *In August 2003 five influential Brazilians went on trial for the torture, mutilation and murder of five children, aged 8 to 13.*

But these were only sample charges, because the men had com-mitted a series of crimes that dated back to 1989. It is thought that there had been as many as 19 victims in total, including the five who had died as a result of the mutilations. Three had survived with horrific injuries, five were never found and six had miraculously escaped. It was not just the barbarity of the crimes that shocked Brazilian society but the fact that four of the accused were highly-educated, professional men. Two were doctors, one was a police officer and the fourth was a re-spectable businessman. The fifth member of the group was cut from different cloth. Valentina de Andrade was a fortune-tell-er and the head of Lineamiento Universal Superior (LUS), a cult that supposedly made contact with extra-terrestrial beings. She was tried for the crimes but not convicted. All of the ac-cused had attempted to use their influence to intimidate wit-nesses and destroy evidence and two were accused of having used their victims' organs in black magic rituals. They may well have done so, but the primary motivation, it appears, was the sadistic sexual abuse of the children and the selling of their organs.

- *In May 1996 three teenage 'Satanists' in San Louis Obispo, California, lured 15-year-old Elyse Pahler to her death with the promise of marijuana. They then strangled and stabbed her before raping the corpse, in the belief that a 'virgin sacrifice' would persuade the devil to bless their Death Metal band, Ha-tred. The three received prison sentences of 26 years to life while their Heavy Metal heroes, Slayer, and their label, faced a lawsuit from the grieving parents, who claimed the band in-cited their mentally-disturbed fans to commit murder.*

Satan is Innocent

These cases are just a small sample of the crimes that have been cited as examples of a widespread Satanic or occult conspiracy. On closer investigation they are revealed to be yet more incidents of sadistic or sociopathic behaviour. It would be naïve, misleading and highly irresponsible to dismiss the possibility that there might be groups who are actively involved in Satanic practices. They might even force unwilling victims to participate in their rituals or commit murder in the devil's name. However, the motives for most of the cases of abuse that the media condemns as 'Satanic' are invariably sadism, sex or a need to control and dominate. The references to Satanism at the time of the crime are merely a way of justifying the criminal act.

If John Lennon was right and there's no heaven above us and no hell below us then hell must be a state of mind of our own making, right here on earth. The parents of three 8-year-old murder victims in West Memphis, Tennessee, knew that this man-made hell was a reality on the morning of 6 May 1993, when the bodies of their sons were found face down in a drainage ditch in Robin Hood Hills, a wooded area just off the interstate highway.

The West Memphis Three

Horrific rumours started circulating as soon as news of the deaths reached town. It was said that the three young friends – Chris Byers, Michael Moore and Stevie Branch – had been mutilated and Satanic symbols had been discovered near the scene. In fact, the boys had not been disfigured at all. They had been stripped naked, hogtied with their own shoelaces and then bludgeoned to death. There was no indication that these had been ritualistic killings.

Nevertheless the rumours persisted. They were fuelled by the local media, who were obsessed with occult killings and so were determined to find devil worshippers behind every evil deed. With no clues to work with, the West Memphis Police Department decided to call in FBI profilers from the Behavioral Science Unit at Quantico, Virginia, but the FBI had little to add except to assure the local investigators that there was no evidence of occultism in the murderer's MO (*modus operandi*). As pressure intensified on the local police to make an arrest, the department turned to West Memphis juvenile officer Jerry Driver, who had been keeping an eye on several individuals who did not conform to the community's image of a good citizen.

The West Memphis Three: Jessie Misskelley, Damien Echols and Jason Baldwin.

Lack of Evidence

With their antisocial attitude and their addiction to Heavy Metal and goodness knows what else, 17-year-old Jessie Misskelley, 16-year-old Jason Baldwin, and 18-year-old Damien Echols looked good for the crime. Had they been regular churchgoers with GI crew cuts and a taste for beer and baseball, it is safe to say that they would never have been suspected. But once the police started probing into their backgrounds, and particularly when they searched Echols' and Baldwin's homes and found a stash of occult literature, their presumptions and prejudices were confirmed.

Even before his arrest, Damien heard the townspeople pointing him out to their friends and neighbours as one of the youths responsible for the killings. Although there was no forensic evidence to connect the three teenagers to the crime scene or to the bodies, the police hauled them in and subjected them to an intense and prolonged grilling. After an unrelenting psychological assault that deprived him of sleep, Jessie finally confessed. He made a statement describing how Damien and Jason had abused the children as part of a Satanic ritual, but it was riddled with inconsistencies. The fact that he was also diagnosed as borderline retarded was not taken into account. Jessie might have been 17 years old at the time, but his mental age was far lower than that.

When Damien heard of the confession he admitted to feeling powerless, angry and frightened. He had good reason to be. Despite a lack of physical proof the West Memphis Three, as they became known, were convicted on a mixture of circumstantial and hearsay evidence. When a knife was recovered from a lake behind Jason's home, expert witnesses testified that it could have made the wounds found on the bodies, yet it was almost certainly not the murder weapon. Recently the wounds were re-examined by seven prominent forensic pathologists, who agreed unanimously that they had been caused by animals after the boys' deaths.

It was also claimed that Damien had been heard confessing to the crime, but he later admitted that he had no recollection of having said such a thing. Even if he had, he said, it would have been mere bravado. More damning was the incredible inefficiency of the police force. In spite of the fact that they had received a report that a man covered in blood and mud had staggered into a fast food restaurant on the night of the murder, they had failed to apprehend him. Not only that, they had managed to lose the blood sample they had recovered from the scene of the crime, according to defence attorney Dan Stidham.

Never Trust an Expert

Damien, Jessie and Jason were subsequently found guilty and Damien was sentenced to death. His friends each received a life sentence. All maintained their innocence.

Damien had been sitting on death row for 16 years, with the prospect of that final walk to the death chamber haunting him day and night, but he had remained optimistic that the truth would eventually surface. And then a miracle took place. Not the one that he had hoped for – the unmasking of the real killer – but an event that should bring that day closer. Hollywood film star Johnny Depp added his name to the list of celebrities who were calling for a review of the case. The fate of the three accused had been sealed by the testimony of Dale Griffis, a highly dubious 'expert witness' on the subject of the occult. Defence attorney Stidham had attempted to discredit him by claiming that he had 'a mail order Ph.D', but no one listened. Griffis testified that the murders were ritual killings because they took place on a night of the full moon and there was a lack of blood at the scene. That revealed the presence of Satanists, he said, because they siphoned blood off so they could drink it or bathe in it. However, no blood was found at the homes of the accused. This placed the burden of proof firmly on the shoulders of the defence. Damien had to deny that he was a Satanist, but his arrogant manner condemned him in the eyes of the jury. 'I had come to feel absolutely hated and loathed by the world,' he later told a reporter.

Denied a Retrial

Then an HBO TV documentary, *Paradise Lost*, raised awareness of the case and highlighted serious flaws in the investigation and the trial. Damien credits the film with having saved his life by raising the prospect of a retrial and encouraging high-profile celebrities such as Johnny Depp to campaign on his behalf. 'I really do believe without that footage of the trials, the state would've probably already killed me by now.' Depp immediately felt an affinity with Damien. Both men had been raised in a small town and both had been condemned as 'freaks' by their conservative neighbours, because of the way they dressed and kept to themselves.

'I can empathize with being judged on how you look,' Depp told an interviewer, 'as opposed to who you are ... My biggest fear ... is that justice is not served, not only for those three innocent men in prison, but also for those three innocent boys.'

Had the accused men sexually abused their victims it is certain that their DNA would have been recovered from the murder scene, even allowing for the cleansing effects of the water in which the boys' bodies were immersed. But no DNA had been found on the corpses or at the location of the crime. Also, FBI profiler John Douglas stated that the profiles of the accused did not match that of the perpetrator. The boys' bikes, clothes and bodies were hidden, which indicates that an adult was responsible – someone who personally knew the victims. After Douglas filed his report, lawyers for the accused submitted further evidence for forensic analysis in the form of two hairs found at the scene. One was found on one of the ligatures that was used to secure the victims and the other was discovered on a nearby tree stump. It was alleged that the first hair matches a DNA sample given by Terry Hobbs, the stepfather of one of the victims, and the other matches that of his friend David Jacoby, who is believed to have been with him on the day of the murder. Jacoby provided Hobbs with his alibi.

On 19 August 2011 Echols, Baldwin and Misskelley were freed after 18 years in jail due to the doubts raised by the DNA evidence. A deal with the authorities meant that they could claim innocence, while agreeing prosecutors had enough evidence to convict them. Meanwhile Johnny Depp took out an option on Damien Echols' forthcoming memoir about the case.

KONSTANTINOS – LUCIFER RISING

The Satanic Rites of Dracula would have been an unremarkable Hammer horror film if the studio had not had the bright idea of setting the story in the present day, with Dracula (played by Christopher Lee) recast as the chief executive of a sinister multinational corporation. Gone were the Gothic trappings – the cobwebbed castle in the Carpathians, the billowing cloak and the horse-drawn hearse to be replaced by a modern penthouse apartment and a Savile Row-suited count, with a brood of leather-clad bikers as his henchmen. The symbolism was obvious but effective. Big business was a heartless enterprise run by anonymous blood-sucking money men.

The same could be said for the way in which Satanism has re-branded itself for the new millennium. Gone are the Gothic theatrical rituals, the altar, the skulls and the sacrificial victim. It has all been replaced by a cool scholarly philosophy in which rituals are visualized in the mind as internal psychodramas for psychological transformation. Satanism is now an intellectual concept or an alternative lifestyle choice, not a cheap horror movie. It's all in the mind and that, of course, is where Satan has been since the beginning. The high priest of this New Age counter-culture/underground movement is a New York neopagan who goes by the name of Konstantinos. Although he draws upon 'nocturnal energies' in his rites and rituals, he is not averse to appearing in broad daylight when he is lecturing on the paranormal at colleges and bookstores or appearing on talk shows to promote his many books. These include *Vampires: The Occult Truth, Summoning Spirits: The Art of Magical Evocation, Speak with the Dead: 7 Methods for Spirit Communication, Gothic Grimoire, Nocturnal Witchcraft* and *The Nocturnicon: Calling Dark Forces and Powers.*

All in the Mind

With a bachelor's degree in journalism and technical writing from New York Polytechnic Institute, Konstantinos is well qualified to serve as a spokesman for a new generation of Satanists weened on *Buffy, the Vampire Slayer* and the *Twilight* movies.

The techniques, imagery and archetypes for conjuring and controlling primal energies will be familiar to anyone who has read Lovecraft's horror fiction or dipped into popular books on Wicca, dream symbolism, Jungian psychology or Crowley's sex magic. As a contemporary Satanist, Konstantinos is not entirely immersed in arcane rites for summoning spirits or communing with the dead. He also finds time for nature magic, banishing unwanted energy from his home (presumably after a visit from the Jehovah's Witnesses or the in-laws) and conquering addiction. He even claims to have cured himself of a brain tumour which was verified before and after an MRI scan. 'Dark workings', he assures his readers, are not 'evil' but designed to put the initiate in contact with 'powerful emotional forces' – in other words, themselves. In fact, close study of his philosophy reveals a closet Goth rather than a traditional Satanist. The dark gods and goddesses that he asks his readers to invoke are no more than projections of their shadow selves and the spirits he encourages them to summon are the thought-forms made manifest from their collective fears.

He urges those who are instinctively drawn to the night, but are wary of invoking forces they fear, to consider the magical process like a computer graphics program and themselves as designers. First they must draw up a blueprint in virtual reality (the astral plane) by visualizing what they desire in considerable detail. They must then give it life by investing it with their mental energy, which can manipulate matter at a subatomic level. Wishing for what you want, it seems, is not enough. The ritual enables you to focus on the desired result to the exclusion of all else, including self-doubt, after which the image is released into the ether, where the universal forces are able to bring it into being. For those who dismiss ritual magic as abstract, unnatural or simply illogical, one could draw a parallel between the magical process and the way in which iron filings form a pattern determined by the poles of a magnet.

Magic and science can be seen as two different disciplines working towards the same end – an understanding of how the universe works and how we can manipulate matter and energy to achieve a desired effect. It is surely only a matter of time before science and the supernatural are reconciled and all psychic phenomena are seen as an extension of the natural world and its laws, rather than a contradiction of them. In subatomic systems, particles retain their connection regardless of how much time and space distance them from the source. So it is with human beings, who retain their connection with the forces that created the universe. As Konstantinos observes, science has only recently discovered the element of dark energy that permeates the fabric of the universe and our being. It connects us with every living thing in existence, although we are not conscious of this during the day, when we are focused on the mundane and material necessities of life. But at night we can more readily quieten the restless mind and connect with this dark energy and its source. Whether we visualize this as a benign god, an indifferent creator or 'an insane agent of chaos', we are all a reflection of it and that makes us 'little gods'. As such we all have access to infinite power. The 'trick' is to wake up and accept that fact and then learn how to connect with it.

If this is the authentic voice of the new Satanism, then there is surely hope that one day we might finally free ourselves of the fear of our own shadow.

ACKNOWLEDGEMENTS

The author gratefully acknowledges the following as primary sources of information:

Baker, Phil, 'The Devil Rides Out – How Dennis Wheatley Sold Black Magic To Britain', article in the *Fortean Times*, January 2010

Cavendish, Richard, *The Black Arts* (Pan Books, 1969)

King, Francis X., *Satan and the Swastika* (Granada, 1976)

LaVey, Anton, *The Satanic Bible* (Avon Books, 1969)

Roland, Paul, *The Nazis and the Occult* (Arcturus, 2006)

Suster, Gerald, *Hitler and the Age of Horus* (Sphere, 1981)

Wheatley, Dennis, *The Devil and All His Works* (Arrow Books, 1973)

Wilson, Colin, *Witches* (Paper Tiger, 1989)

Internet Resources:

www.geraldgardner.com

http://en.wikipedia.org/wiki/Alan_Moore

INDEX

INDEX

INDEX